The
Year
of the
Poet X

June 2023

The Poetry Posse

inner child press, ltd.

The Poetry Posse 2023

Gail Weston Shazor
Shareef Abdur Rasheed
Teresa E. Gallion
hülya n. yılmaz
Kimberly Burnham
Tzemin Ition Tsai
Elizabeth Esguerra Castillo
Jackie Davis Allen
Joe Paire
Caroline 'Ceri' Nazareno
Ashok K. Bhargava
Alicja Maria Kuberska
Swapna Behera
Albert 'Infinite' Carrasco
Michelle Joan Barulich
Eliza Segiet
William S. Peters, Sr.

~ * ~

In order to maintain each poet's authentic voice, this volume has not undergone the scrutiny of editing. Please take time to indulge each contributor for their own creativity and aspirations to convey their uniqueness.

hülya n. yılmaz, Ph.D.
Director of Editing ~
Inner Child Press International

The Year of the Poet X
June 2023 Edition

The Poetry Posse

1st Edition : 2023

Publisher Information
1st Edition : Inner Child Press
intouch@innerchildpress.com
www.innerchildpress.com

WHAT WOULD LIFE BE WITHOUT A LITTLE POETRY?

Dedication

This Book is dedicated to

Humanity, Peace & Poetry

the Power of the Pen

can effectuate change!

&

The Poetry Posse

past, present & future,

our Patrons and Readers &

the Spirit of our Everlasting Muse

In the darkness of my life
I heard the music
I danced . . .
and the Light appeared
and I dance

Janet P. Caldwell

Table of Contents

The Poetry Posse

Table of Contents . . . *continued*

June's Featured Poets   111

Inner Child Press News   141

Other Anthological Works   177

Foreword
Children: Difference Makers

Ryan Hreljac

"Jus give me cool drink of water fore I die" Ms. Maya said.

And sometimes it is just that. The need to quench a longing for something so basic in life that we can't imagine living without it. Water is a basic component of living. Everything around us, including us, is made up of large amounts of water. We cannot survive without it.

The access to this life sustaining element, although essential, is often unavailable to large populations on the earth. Given man's proclivity to pollution, containment and even hoarding has created a world where we must go in search of water. Where rivers once flowed now sit houses and factories. Where waterfalls were once free to carve paths across our landscapes, we have created man-made recreational parks and such where the privilege can go to see what we have prohibited to the poor.

Our featured free thinker and doer has understood what many have not. We need to ensure that water and other necessities are available for everyone. It may take one to plant a seed of refreshment. It may take many to dig a well. It may take a government to break a dam. It will take a world to turn back the environment.

What we don't have is the luxury of letting someone die for a cool drink of water. Needs cannot always be a desire.

Gail Weston Shazor

Author ~ Artist ~ Humanitarian

$\mathcal{P}$reface

We, **Inner Child Press International, The Year of the Poet** and **The Poetry Posse** welcome you.

We are so excited as we are now offer unto you our sixth month of our **10th** year of monthly publication of this enterprise, **The Year of the Poet**.

For those of you who are not familiar with our story, back in 2013, a few of us poets got together with the simple intention of producing a book a month. That was our challenge. Since that time the enterprise has blossomed and brought forth a fruit that seems to keep on growing as evidenced as we enter 2023.

Our purpose is simple. Through our lyrical words and verse, we not only wish to share our poetic works, but we also have the poetic naiveté to believe that we can assist in the growth of consciousness of the things that have an effect our collective humanity. Therefore, we welcome your readership. For more about what we are attempting to accomplish, have a look at our Publishing Web Site . . . www.innerchildpress.com. If you would like to know a bit more about this particular endeavor please stop by for a visit at :
www.innerchildpress.com/the-year-of-the-poet

Over the years, Inner Child Press has been socially active to bring awareness and catalog through literature the things that have an impact upon our world and its inhabitants. We have solicited, produced, underwritten and published quite a few volumes to that end. For more insight you may wish to visit : www.innerchildpress.com/the-anthology-market. If you are a writer, poet, or activist, you would be advised to keep a eye out for upcoming volumes should you desire to participate. All readers are welcomed as well. Note, that there is a myriad of published volumes that are available as a FREE PDF download as well as available for purchase at affordable prices.

We at this time extend to you our well wishes for your own personal journey and hope that you consider including us as a travel companion.

Bless Up

Bill

William S. Peters, Sr.

Publisher
Inner Child Press International
www.innerchildpress.com

Children
Difference Makers
Ryan Hreljac
June 2023

by Kimberly Burnham, Ph.D.

Hreljac has been working to make clean water accessible to people in poor areas since he was six and first learned about the issue. He began by doing chores to earn money to send to organizations building wells in poor countries before starting Ryan's Well Foundation when he was 10. The charity has brought drinkable water to over 800,000 people in 16 countries. Ryan's Well Foundation also partners with schools to educate children about the situation.

"Freshwater is but a small fraction – about 2.5% - of the total water on Earth. Precipitation is the ultimate source of freshwater. If the world's water fit into a bucket, only one teaspoonful would be drinkable. 864 million people lack access to an improved water supply - approximately one in six people on earth. 2.5 billion people in the world do not have access to adequate sanitation; this is roughly two fifths of the world's population. Millions of women and children spend several hours a day collecting water from distant, often polluted sources. Almost two in three people lacking access to clean water live on less than $2 a day. Globally, more than 125 million children under five years of age live in households without access to an improved drinking-water source, and more than 280 million children under five live in households without access to improved sanitation facilities." ~Ryan's Well Foundation

Poets . . .
sowing seeds in the
Conscious Garden of Life,
that those who have yet to come
may enjoy the Flowers.

Poets, Writers . . . know that we are the enchanting magicians that nourishes the seeds of dreams and thoughts . . . it is our words that entice the hearts and minds of others to believe there is something grand about the possibilities that life has to offer and our words tease it forth into action . . . for you are the Poet, the Writer to whom the Gift of Words has been entrusted . . .

~ wsp

poetry is . . .

Poetry succeeds where instruction fails.

~ wsp

Now Available

Inner Child Press International
&
The Year of the Poet
present

Poetry

the best of 2022

Poets of the World

innerchildpressanthologies@gmail.com

Gail Weston Shazor

This is a creative promise ~ my pen will speak to and for the world. Enamored with letters and respectful of their power, I have been writing for most of my life. A mother, daughter, sister and grandmother I give what I have been given, greatfilledly.

Author of . . .

"An Overstanding of an Imperfect Love"
&
Notes from the Blue Roof

Lies My Grandfathers Told Me

available at Inner Child Press.

www.facebook.com/gailwestonshazor
www.innerchildpress.com/gail-weston-shazor
navypoet1@gmail.com

Bearer

Mother Rain called me from sleep just now
She sent the wind to whisper across coconut fronds
Of her impending arrival
My pillow no longer soothing
I rose to answer
It had been far too long since we greeted
Unimpeded and natural under a night sky
With just a thought to a towel
I tiptoed out in joyous solemnity
Without hesitation to submerge into
The capturedness of her
Cool, inviting we waited together
On the wildness to come
My limbs drifting lightly
My back settled against the stone
Gracefully
Greatfilledly
Gently
As I faced the heavens
And then she came
The water bearer for whom I was born
With enough to cover all
In refreshingness
In the loudness of cleansing
I felt so
Until my skin felt new
Until the weariness washed away
Until my soul felt eased
I gave it all to her
And she accepted unconditionally
The things I no longer had need of
I stood under the wet without fear

While the ghosts behind
The mist stained glass
Danced in time to a music
That only they could hear.

Fading Memories

i can't remember
i have tried to call to recall
just how you smelled
on the day that i handed you
your very first grandson
i can't remember just how your
mouth moved to form a smile
my hands touch my face often
but it doesn't feel
like i don't remember you did
i panick at the thought
that soon, probably sooner
than anyone can even imagine
i will not think of you
with this pain
and i will only think of you
when that girl child cusses
and my sister laughs
and the aunt tells the stories
of the baby sister she loved
and then the time will come
when it's only the holidays
when i long for you
to make the dressing and greens
but my sister will make it for me
and it will taste the same
but different
and I will long the same
but different
and i panick every time
i lose another memory
of what our hands looked like
held together

Watch me Now

I always wonder if
The pieces of ink
I have tucked away
In the short corners
Of where wall meets floor
And the memory speaks
Will find their way
Out into the open life
And will you hear me
In broken English and
Broken wants for this companion
And I picked up today
That things happen when
They are supposed to
But what if
We don't recognize
The sup-position?
You speak to me around
The words you choose to
Want to need to share
And I hear you
In the small voices
Even though it is a strain
To decipher the warning
From the laughter
"Watch me now"
And I do
For both the instruction
And the caution
So i fall back to the corner
Of where the wall
Meets the floor

Wrapping the syntax
That I have gathered
Of small snippets of words
Around the silvering hair
That I now possess
And I wonder
If ink is a proving ground

Alicja Maria Kuberska

Alicja Maria Kuberska

Alicja Maria Kuberska – awarded Polish poetess, novelist, journalist, editor.

She is a member of the Polish Writers Associations in Warsaw, Poland and IWA Bogdani, Albania. She is also a member of directors' board of Soflay Literature Foundation, Our Poetry Archive (India) and Cultural Ambassador for Poland (Inner Child Press, USA)

Her poems have been published in numerous anthologies and magazines in : Poland, Czech Republic, Slovakia, Hungary,Ukraina, Belgium, Bulgaria, Albania, Spain, the UK, Italy, the USA, Canada, the UK, Argentina, Chile, Peru, Israel, Turkey, India, Uzbekistan, South Korea, Taiwan, China, Australia, South Africa, Zambia, Nigeria

She received two medals - the Nosside UNESCO Competition in Italy (2015) and European Academy of Science Arts and Letters in France (2017). Ahe also received a reward of international literary competition in Italy „ Tra le parole e 'elfinito" (2018). She was announced a poet of the 2017 year by Soflay Literature Foundation (2018).She also received : Bolesław Prus Prize Poland (2019), Culture Animator Poland (2019) and first prize Premio Internazionale di Poesia Poseidonia- Paestrum Italy (2019).

Ryan Hreljac
Life-giving water

In the desert,
the cracked soil begs for a downpour
The cloudless sky is sparse in rain
Clouds follow different paths
and they rarely dance above the gray land.

The merciful mother Earth gives people
the gift of oases and underground rivers.
Artesian wells make dreams come true
about clean water and fertility.

Everyone can help and like a child
offer a thirsty man
one drop of clean water
and hope for a better fate

Collegiate church in Kruszwica

In the autumn gilt of leaves,
on the banks of lake Gopło,
the stone collegiate church fell asleep.

Time stopped at the threshold of the temple.
It doesn't go inside
and freezes motionless.

It paused the hands of the clock
so that everything will continue
as it was centuries ago
- in the ancient beauty of history.

The lake tells legends and myths
about mice in the tower and nymphs,
It plays stories with waves.

The wind weaves in the twigs of forked willows
the words from Przybyszewski' s diary
about nostalgia and autumn sadness.

The church far from the city
does not follow the rhythm of life.
It is rooted in history.

I come and go.
I touch the mighty walls.
I am a fleeting moment.

afternoon with mom

a summer day blooms in an old photograph
a smiling girl is sitting on a stone
she has a meadow bouquet of wildflowers
chamomile petals whisper to her
a fortune about her beloved

on the next one a happy couple in the park
is walking together into the future
there is a little sun between them
their mystery of the black nights

next to me an old woman in an armchair
has faded eyes without hope
look at these pictures mom
time has stolen everything from you
and over a half from me

Jackie
Davis
Allen

Jackie Davis Allen, otherwise known as Jacqueline D. Allen or Jackie Allen, grew up in the Cumberland Mountains of Appalachia. As the next eldest daughter of a coal miner father and a stay at home mother, she was the first in her family to attend and graduate from college. Her siblings, in their own right, are accomplished, though she is the only one, to date, that has discovered the gift of writing.

Graduating from Radford University, with a Bachelor's of Science degree in Early Education, she taught in both public and private schools. For over a decade she taught private art classes to children both in her home and at a local Art and Framing Shop where she also sold her original soft sculptured Victorian dolls and original christening gowns.

She resides in northern Virginia with her husband, taking much needed get-aways to their mountain home near the Blue Ridge Mountains, a place that evokes memories of days spent growing up in the Appalachian Mountains.

A lover of hats, she has worn many. Following marriage to her college sweetheart, and as wife, mother, grandmother, teacher, tutor, artist, writer, poet and crafter, she is a lover of art and antiques, surrounding herself, always, with books, seeking to learn more.

In 2015 she authored *Looking for Rainbows, Poetry, Prose and Art*, and in 2017, *Dark Side of the Moon*. Both books of mostly narrative poetry were published by Inner Child Press and were edited by hulya n. yilmaz in 2019, *No Illusions. Through the Looking Glass*, which was nominated to be considered for a Pulitzer Prize by the publisher and editor of Inner Child Press, ltd.

http://www.innerchildpress.com/jackie-davis-allen.php
jackiedavisallen.com

Water, Water

Friends, neighbors, family,
In need of water.
In need of money.
Needing clean water to drink.

Organized actions help
The poor, they who like me, in need
Of wells; like what I remember
From my own youthful days.

From effort, from passion
The dream fulfilled,
Not just with the little of insufficient funds
But also from life's need and effort.

Without clean water,
What is life?
Without ideas, needs,
What are dreams?

Without action, effort,
The status quo remains.
With purposeful intention, action,
Dreams manifest themselves.

Clean water, ah, clean water!
Satisfaction for mankind.
For the physical thirst, but also
For the spiritual thirst. For survival.

Island Music

I can hear the island music,
The waves gently slapping
And sliding against the beach,
The sun slowly slipping down
From and into the blue.
I see her golden grace
Embracing the earth,
Speaking to me.
Yet making not a sound.
Beautiful is the vision,
That is but a figment
Of my imagination.
Even still it comforts me.
It is where I go
In turbulent and troubled times,
To meditate and reflect
Upon God's blessings, and to consider
His goodness to mankind.
Away from my island of rest
And far too near to my residence,
Afoul presence of evil attempts
To destroy, with malice,
The flowers that desire only to be.
Despite the clamor that would
Drown out the music,
I lift up my voice.
And pray for peace.

The Sultry Hours of Longing

Here I am, stuck in the same old place,
A stubborn briar festering and aching
From choices made, without thinking.

Though some did prick my conscious
And the sting, lo, it is still with me;
Yet it, I ignored...

The warning signs for the heat
Of the night fell upon me;
And there in the moonlight garden,

Anticipation was so enticing
To the eyes, to the taste,
And to the feeling.

And savoring it,
Yes, savoring it,
I was overcome...

Stricken by the longing,
The passion of its bliss,
I fell into the forbidden tryst.

And, lo, I am aching for more...
Another taste of your lips,
For more of your touch.

I am longing for one more dream like this.

Tzemin
Ition
Tsai

Tzemin Ition Tsai

Dr. Tzemin Ition Tsai comes from the Republic of China(Taiwan). In addition to being a professor of literature at a university, he is more committed to writing poems, novels, and proses. He is also an editor of "Reading, Writing and Teaching" academic text, an International editor of "Contemporary dialogues" literary periodical in Macedonia, and Vice-Chairman of the International Jury of the SAHITTO INTERNATIONAL AWARD in Bangladesh, and a columnist for "Chinese Language Monthly" in Taiwan.

In a wide range of literary creations, he is particularly fond of interesting stories or novels, and writing articles or poems about the feelings of nature and human beings. He has won many national literary awards. His literary works have been anthologized and published in books, journals, and newspapers in more than 55 countries and have been translated into more than 24 languages.

Autumn Water

Now, the weather has just
Turned into sunny
The old fisherman stands alone, bent arms cast a pair of
cuffs
Beg for fish but not for wind
Not at all afraid of the past diving into the waves of smoke
Only want to ask, which hometown is the most memorable?
Why don't let the fish tired of swimming tell me
Carrying a jug of wine with spray, loosen my hair
A sea hibiscus, poked
Everything is so casual, why does this
Always happen when the autumn water is not awake?

Dare to ask the geese that are returning home
But dare not ask the depths of my heart, unbearable
To be cut off by autumn, my
Depression after the loss of whirling and scattering
Fishing fire determines dusk
Listening vaguely to the turbulent sound of the waves
Lazy walk, don't be sentimental
Getting away from the tsundere of autumn water
White hair frost have no intention of understanding
However, pointed out everything all in that sneer

The Old Fisherman

The morning light pierces this dawn
In the distance, a lonely boat dangles on the water
At the bottom of the spring river, the old fisherman
Only correspond his shadow to the willow
Occasionally, a few birds on the beach
A few soft sounds, entrained
The white flower spiral on the water surface of the catkins,
no longer fly
That old fisherman pull back his sparse white hair
Behold, how the peak draws sorrow?
A heart calm and not intoxicated
The sound of water waves in the mangrove hypnotizes
In a half-dream, talk about the price of perch
If not greedy the silence recommended by running water
fish fat
The laughter in the village flows out
Since, far away from the cock crowing and noise
With a jug of wine and a threw-hook
Neither can find any fish
Other than, inviting the howling wind come to fish together
What can he do?

Looking Back At My Youth

Recall
How many years?
That non-returning departure
Today
Riding the wind and singing wildly, broken my flute
Cherry blossoms all over the street but don't want to get
drunk with me
Drunk in
The irreversible flowing water
The wild and unrestrained trail of the past that cannot be
traced back
Also, can't chase back my temples which gray as autumn

If I know
Young never again
Have to grow old to swallow clouds and draw out dreams?
Buy ridicule with the spring breeze
Fell down laughing
Poor until everything is forgotten
Maybe nothing at all is enough to forget everything
To make a name can't replace
That disheartened, outside the green window
That's not like my life should be

Shareef
Abdur
Rasheed

Shareef Abdur Rasheed

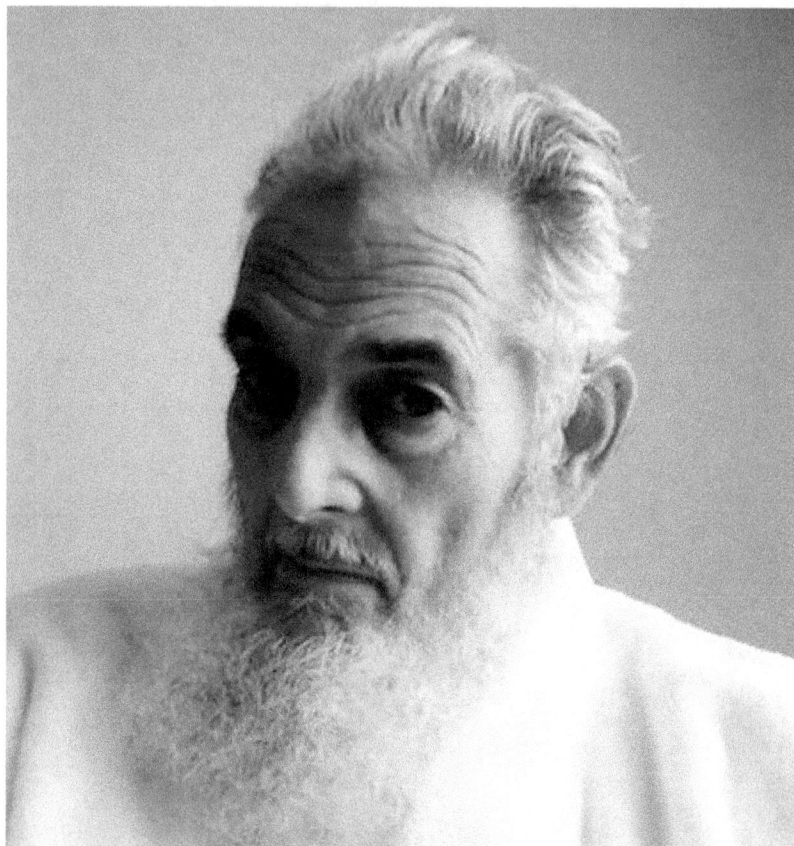

Shareef Abdur-Rasheed, AKA Zakir Flo was born and raised in Brooklyn, New York. His education includes Brooklyn College, Suffolk County Community College and Makkah, Saudi Arabia. He is a Veteran of the Viet Nam era, where in 1969 he reverted to his now reverently embraced Islamic Faith. He is very active in the Islamic community and beyond with his teachings, activism and his humanity.

Shareef's spiritual expression comes through the persona of "Zakir Flo" . Zakir is Arabic for "To remind". Never silent, Shareef Abdur-Rasheed is always dropping science, love, consciousness and signs of the time in rhyme.

Shareef is the Patriarch of the Abdur-Rasheed Family with 9 Children (6 Sons and 3 Daughters) and 41 Grandchildren (24 Boys and 17 Girls).

For more information about Shareef, visit his personal FaceBook Page at :

https://www.facebook.com/shareef.abdurrasheed1
https://zakirflo.wordpress.com

Ryan Hreljac

Ryan Hreljac 6 years old
discovered in Africa
numerous countries
struggled to have clean
drinking water
he collected as much
money as he could
doing chores
eventually he collected
$2,000.00 which was
enough to build a well
in Africa
he connected with a non-
profit organization that builds
wells that provide clean water
in poor countries that was the
first well drilled in Northern
Uganda built by Canadian
Physicians for Aid and Relief
in just 2 years this 8-year-old
Canadian boy raised $61,000
The Canadian International
Development Agency who
became aware of Ryan's
dedicated efforts matched $2.00
to every $1.00 the young boy
raised
he founded a foundation named
after him
a registered Canadian charity

Ryan's Well Foundation
goal build wells across the globe
where clean water was hard to
find
His foundation has to date made
it possible for almost a million
people to have clean water
spread out over 16 countries
never underestimate what a
child can achieve

Ability

of an underlying force conducting,
putting pieces in place, constructing
never in haste setting the pace
directing the fate of human race
inspecting current events one can not
conclude by logically coming to an explanation
truly because it's simply prophecy being played
as not to let the sensationalism fool ya
cast of characters in this production will change
inevitably that's the consistency of prophecy
they all have parts to play so pray every day
that their parts don't steal hearts away
or souls stole, sold or even given away
getting caught up in the hype of the play
performed on the world stage everyday
characters portrayed are never what they seem
there is much more to this picture then appears
on the screen know what i mean
today the role of Pharaoh is played by orange face
with " HUGE " payroll
tomorrow who knows Answer: only the creator,
orchestrater, coordinator, originator wrote the script
with the first creation the pen
ink is dried, pen laid down and the play goes on
as written and the players that do their parts
are temporary but the play always remains
contemporary
no matter what day, hour players play their parts never
have power to flip the real script or even to quit until it
appears in the script
sounds complicated
to understand the script
ask the playwright

murder

bullS#!+ drive bye's
let it fly eyeballs high
then dem die and don't know why
cee?
cause dem lived in the information nation
so much information caused massive
mind, heart, soul inflammation
riddled with rounds of bull$#!+
massive become misfits
dem passive medicated by the gases emanated
left only flashes of consciousness motivated
not enough to possess substance
rather than the bull$#! dumped on us
death by bull$#!+ but instead of
bury the dead dem bury the lie instead
unconscious living dead zombies remain
amongst us

Kimberly Burnham

Kimberly Burnham

A brain health expert with a PhD in Integrative Medicine, Kimberly Burnham has lived in tropical Colombia; in Belgium during the Vietnam War; in Japan teaching businessmen English; in diverse international Toronto, Canada; and several places in the US. Now, she's in Spokane, WA with her wife, Elizabeth, two sets of twins (age 11 & 14) and three dogs. Her recent book, *Awakenings: Peace Dictionary, Language and the Mind, a Daily Brain Health Program* includes the word for peace in hundreds of languages. Her poetry weaves through 80+ volumes of *The Year of the Poet, Inspired by Gandhi, Women Building the World*, and *A Woman's Place in the Dictionary*. She is currently working on several ekphrastic writing projects. One is a novel, *Art Thief Cracks Healing Code for Parkinson's Disease* and the other is non-fiction, *Using Ekphrastic Fiction Writing and Poetry to Create Interest and Promote Artists, Writers, and Poets*.

http://www.NerveWhisperer.Solutions

https://healthy-brain.medium.com/bears-at-the-window-of-climate-change-d1fb403eeaf3

Lucky Well Water

I come into my cool house
from the 90-degree heat outside in the garden
weeding is tough
watering the plants is easier
the plant I want grow in the sunlight sustained
by water from my well
I feel lucky
I have a well to nourish the beauty around me
to drink from the tap
to shower after a day outside gardening

Ryan's Well

At six he looks around his classroom

imagines others far away

dreams of the water they drink in doom

changes the world and what we say

Blood

Sea salts my veins

I can't drink an ocean but

must pray for clean rain

Elizabeth E. Castillo

Elizabeth Esguerra Castillo

Elizabeth Esguerra Castillo is a multi-awarded and an Internationally-Published Contemporary Author/Poet and a Professional Writer / Creative Writer / Feature Writer / Journalist / Travel Writer from the Philippines. She has 2 published books, "Seasons of Emotions" (UK) and "Inner Reflections of the Muse", (USA). Elizabeth is also a co-author to more than 60 international anthologies in the USA, Canada, UK, Romania, India. She is a Contributing Editor of Inner Child Magazine, USA and an Advisory Board Member of Reflection Magazine, an international literary magazine. She is a member of the American Authors Association (AAA) and PEN International.

Web links:

Facebook Fan Page

https://free.facebook.com/ElizabethEsguerraCastillo

Google Plus

https://plus.google.com/u/0/+ElizabethCastillo

Ryan's Well

At a tender age, Ryan made a stand
A Grade One student at that time,
He already knew the right of African children
To have access to safe drinking water
His innocent mind started to wander
How he can help them in his own little ways
Ryan's well became immortal
Inspired the world to keep drinking water safe
All because of a young kid who already had the heart
To change the world.

Cleansing Rains

Dewey teardrops from heaven above falling
As I reminisce the life before I've been in
Brings me back memories of yesteryears
Of laughter still echoing and overflowing tears.
My heart skips a beat tuning in with your rhythmic sound
Splattering into bits as you melodiously hit the ground
No, it doesn't mean its pain I always think of when you're
here
But also of cleansing my soul of evil demons I wish to
disappear.
A rainbow may soon manifest itself from the distant
horizon
Coloring my world with magical hues giving me inspiration
After you have dared exit from your magnanimous
performance
Giving the stage now to King Sun as another beautiful day
is at a glance!

The Boy by the Waterfalls

I see you in one of my greatest dreamscapes,
Sitting on a huge rock facing the majestic waterfalls
As I emerge out of nowhere in a place called the Ruins,
Where an ancient, mystic castle used to stand tall
A witness to a great kingdom's sweet downfall.
A river runs through the debris of this enchanting
sanctuary,
Flowing from under a magical bridge where I am about to
cross
And there came to view, a vivid and glimmering sight of
you,
But I failed to see how you could have looked
For your back was facing me while you immersed in
soulful serenity.
I missed to behold how your eyes could have stared
beautifully at me
Or if you are lonely and needs someone to be just there to
listen,
As tears flow down your cheeks looking for answers in
beautiful solitude.
I was about to step on the rock you are sitting on to tap
your back and say "Hi!"
But then you vanished into thin air and what was left was
white smoke,
And the empty space you left- the same spot I sat on and
delved into my own contemplation
Then a realization came upon me that you wanted me to
carefully view the waterfalls you have laid your eyes on.
The waterfalls signifying the ebb and flow of life,
Things happen every now and then, constant changes
inevitably take place

Every split second and in the mere blink of an eye,
But life continuously flows come what may
What matters is how we enjoy our journey,
And do not have regrets for what could have been, what
might have been
But simply cherish how things used to be.

Joe
Paire

Joe Paire

Joseph L Paire' aka Joe DaVerbal Minddancer . . .
is a quiet man, born in a time where civil liberties
were a walk on thin ice. He's been a victim of his
own shyness often sidelined in his own quest for
love. He became the observer, charting life's path.
Taking note of the why, people do what they do. His
writings oft times strike a cord with the
dormant strings of the reader. His pen the rosined
bow drawn across the mind. He comes full-frontal
or in the subtlest way, always expressing in a way
that stimulate the senses.

www.facebook.com/joe.minddancer

Aquaman

Ryan Hreljac, here we go with a six-year-old boy.
The story goes: after he learned about the situation, He
earned money doing chores to help fund a well
He's been working to make clean water accessible to
people in poor areas

At Six years old I couldn't fathom or imagine
Doing such a selfless act, at six years old
I gathered and sold soda bottles,
to buy an army man pack; I played outback
I played in dirt, Ryan Hreljac put in work
Midnight walks,
to fetch water for an aunt's well

Ryan Hreljac, sent money to organizations building wells
in poor countries
before starting "Ryan's Well Foundation"
when he was 10.
The charity has brought drinkable water to over 800,000
people in 16 countries.

A true superhero to be sure
Ryan Hreljac, helped the poor
He didn't rob from the rich
He helped fund the wishes,
and the building of wells
to provide water to the many
who didn't have any.
I admire not envy, Ryan Hreljac
The real AQUAMAN at age 10 imagine that.

Artificial Intelligence

Remember the abacus
Remember the slide rule
I remember having to use them in school
I remember being taught,
"You better learn to count your money"
I remember being stuck,
because math wasn't my forte

Enter the calculator, my little cheap Casio
I remember being told,
leave your calculator alone.
A pop quiz in my math class,
I'm feeling a little math-less
Eh! Here comes another zero
Artificial intelligence will not be my hero

The Roman's weren't hearing Nero
I'm not easy to teach so,
Hey, I need my AI, my computer tutor
My educational prime mover
My engine, wherein, I get my where in the world
My engines wearing down, not doing my research
Can Artificial intelligence truly prove it's worth
Cheat codes to be whole,
no experiences, truth be told
Have you artificially sold your soul?
Can you relate to a mate, can you bake a cake?
Can artificially predict your fate?
How's your algorithm feeling today
Remember the abacus and slide rule?
Hey, I remember before AI.

It's Not Impossible

It's not impossible to get along
You just have to want it
Is someone stopping you from being you
Do you really want that
Maybe I'll just take your car,
I'll bet you'll say, "Bump that"

It's not impossible to live in peace
There's probably a leader
Who do both sides listen to
While their citizens lie there bleeding
While their citizens are freezing
While their leaders fail to feed them
Freedom, has always been a joke
You can't even stay woke, awaken, aware

It's not impossible if you care
It's highly probable if you dare take a chance
Have you ever calmed down an angry man
Did you make him listen to what he said
Did you point out the consequences
Of their foolishness, who rules this mess
A fool in gest, and gestures haven't been used,
in a while I bet.

It's not impossible to be a good human
If your philosophy is to be all you could man
What we should and should not
What we could and could not
What we would and would not
It's not impossible to speak the truth out.

hülya

n.

yılmaz

hülya n. yılmaz

Professor Emerita, hülya n. yılmaz is a published author, literary translator, and Co-Chair and Director of Editing Services at Inner Child Press International. Her poetic work appeared in numerous anthologies of global endeavors and was presented at various literary events in the U.S. and abroad. In 2018, WIN honored yılmaz with an award of excellence. Since 2017, her two poems remain permanently installed in *Telepoem Booth* – a U.S.-wide poetic art exhibition. hülya finds it vital for everyone to seek a deeper sense of self, and writes creatively to attain a comprehensive awareness for and development of our humanity.

hülya n. yılmaz, a traveler on the journey called "life" . . .

Writing Web Site
https://hulyanyilmaz.com/

Editing Web Site
https://hulyasfreelancing.com

it is no luxury . . .

to have access to clean water
in developed countries

yet . . .

there is no running water
for approximately 2.2 million Americans,
and inadequate water systems
for about 44 million people in the U.S.A.

. . . as we are close to reaching
the middle of 2023

our politicians, aka our so-called leaders
on one hand;
Ryan Hreljac, on the other

a young individual who cares
not about politics but is rather committed
to serve millions of people
with his Well Foundation program

1,667 water projects and
1,317 latrines . . .
completed in 17 countries,
enabling 1,344,554 people
to have safe water and sanitation

. . . as he, too, is close to reaching
the middle of 2023

Just a Few Words

"Flint Water Crisis"

Michigan, U.S.A.

April 25, 2014 to present

Needed ASAP:

An American Ryan Hreljac!

a child-like imagination

one foot on the ground

the other tip-toed along

her wings took them both

hülya n. yılmaz

Teresa E. Gallion

Teresa E. Gallion was born in Shreveport, Louisiana and moved to Illinois at the age of 15. She completed her undergraduate training at the University of Illinois Chicago and received her master's degree in Psychology from Bowling Green State University in Ohio. She retired from New Mexico state government in 2012.

She moved to New Mexico in 1987. While writing sporadically for many years, in 1998 she started reading her work in the local Albuquerque poetry community. She has been a featured reader at local coffee houses, bookstores, art galleries, museums, libraries, Outpost Performance Space, the Route 66 Festival in 2001 and the State of Oklahoma's Poetry Festival in Cheyenne, Oklahoma in 2004. She occasionally hosts an open mic.

Teresa's work is published in numerous Journals and anthologies. She has two CDs: *On the Wings of the Wind* and *Poems from Chasing Light.* She has published three books: *Walking Sacred Ground, Contemplation in the High Desert* and *Chasing Light.*

Chasing Light was a finalist in the 2013 New Mexico/Arizona Book Awards.

The surreal high desert landscape and her personal spiritual journey influence the writing of this Albuquerque poet. When she is not writing, she is committed to hiking the enchanted landscapes of New Mexico. You may preview her work at

http://bit.ly/1aIVPNq or *http://bit.ly/13IMLGh*

A Legacy of Water

Poor in coins, rich in spirit,
dedicated and committed.
Born to make a mark on planet earth.

Your legacy staked its claim on you
at the age of 6 tender years.
You demonstrated the power

of determination and true grit
with humble beginnings
that led to Ryan's Well.

Clear water still flows
in many countries
because of your legacy of love.

Catch the Wave

The open road is the only opium
you need to experience freedom
trembling in your luscious body.

Ride your rubber wheels on asphalt
and throw kisses to the clouds.
They will speak back to you
in rainbows and water blossoms.

Look, listen and savor every love stimulus
riding the open road beside you.
The sky is falling for you.
Embrace the gift with love notes.

A low rider in the desert
on a highway to nowhere
seeks the still solitude
of desert spaces that call spirit home.

No need to worry about
the distance nor danger.
The desert holds the keys
to your life. Each key
is given when readiness is achieved.

Do not forget to lookup.
The clouds stream messages
in a consensus around your head.
Be vigilant and catch the wave.

Lyrical Release

Sacred syllables ride up my spine
create a flash flood in my brain.
Raging ripples spit wild words.

I want to catch and release
soft baked words of wisdom,
ride sea waves,
float down rivers,
climb majestic mountains
and see the world
as a lake of goodness.

I want to mute all voices
and massage faces
with lyrical phrases
that move mountains to shiver,
grass to sway in open meadows,
rocks to slide down hillsides.

When the sound current of love
slaps me in the face,
may my arms open
and receive sacred lyrics.

Ashok K. Bhargava

ASHOK BHARGAVA is a poet, writer, inspirational speaker and a literary consultant. He has attended poetry conferences in Italy, Turkey, India and Philippines. His latest book "Riding the Tide" about his battle with cancer has been translated and published in Arabic, Hindi, Telugu and Bengali languages. He is a contributing writer to several anthologies worldwide including World Poetry Almanac 2014. He has been published in numerous print and online magazines.

Ashok has won many accolades including Poet Ambassador to Japan, Kalidasa International award, World Poetry Lifetime Achievement award, Writers Beyond Borders Peace award and Tapsilog Leadership award for his community involvement. He is founder of Writers International Network Canada Society to discover, nourish, recognize and celebrate writers, poets and artists and to assist them to network with the community at large. He is the author of eight books of poetry and one anthology. He is Artist-in-Residence at Moberly Arts & Cultural Centre and also co-edits the literary section of The Link Newspaper.

Living Water

Water is in short supply.
The old wells are running dry.

No rain
falling from above
to irrigate fauna and flora
with soaking love.

We get to find
the ways to survive
grow and thrive.

Let's become the pure water
that flows down
the mountain heads of snow
clean and safe to drink
adding to life a sparkling glow.

My quest is to become water
flow merrily
singing
thirst quenching and
life giving.

Poetry of Childhood

Dedicated to the memory of uncle Dine Nath & Uncle Hem Raj

Summer is the sweet smell of blossoms
in my uncle's orchard.

I'd pick up a ripe pink-orange
the best looking mango.

Wash it.

I would not peel it to reveal
it's golden pulp.

Rather I will soften it by rolling
slowly between my palms.

Then I'd nibble a neat hole
at its top
and pull the pulp
up slowly into my mouth.

I'd do this all while
listening to Mukesh (John Denver of India),
on the radio, so that the juice
could fall freely with a melody
into my stomach.

This is the fleeting
poetry of my childhood.

That Moment

(March 24, 2023)

How could one account for it, coming as it did
during the conversation, building itself up

in the back of the mind? anger, it lashed
the tender veins of heart until they exploded,

ripped spires off humility, tumbled walls of love.
Destroying everything that was carefully built. Dignity

was thrown off the sides of mountains.
Caustic words roared in back and forth

ripped through lips, blew emotions
from across the coffee table. The like

had never been seen. It was the start, the
Snapped relations, hurting without healings.

It was a shameful leaving, thrown out.
There was not much left behind

that night — bloodied hearts scattered, sentiments
whipped to shreds, and the love

the foundation of parental privilege
no longer seen. It was a catastrophe.

Caroline
'Ceri Naz'
Nazareno
Gabis

Caroline 'Ceri' Nazareno-Gabis

Caroline 'Ceri Naz' Nazareno-Gabis, author of Velvet Passions of Calibrated Quarks, World Poetry Canada International Director to Philippines is a multi-awarded poet, editor, journalist, educator, peace and women's advocate. She believes that learning other's language and culture is a doorway to wisdom.

Among her poetic belts include **Gabrielle Galloni Memorial Panorama International Youth Award 2022**, Panorama Youth Literary Awards 2020, 7th Prize Winner in the 19th, 20th and 21st Italian Award of Literary Festival; Writers International Network-Canada ''Amazing Poet 2015'', The Frang Bardhi Literary Prize 2014 (Albania), Poet Journalist Award 2014 (Tuzla, Istanbul, Turkey) and World Poetry Empowered Poet 2013 (Vancouver, Canada). She's a featured member of Association of Women's Rights and Development (AWID), The Poetry Posse, Galaktika Poetike, Asia Pacific Writers and Translators (APWT), Axlepino and Anacbanua. Her poetry and children's stories have been featured in different anthologies and magazines worldwide.

Links to her works:

http://panitikan.ph/2018/03/30/caroline-nazareno-gabis/

https://apwriters.org/author/ceri_naz/

http://www.aveviajera.org/nacionesunidasdelasletras/id1181.html

One Well, Water of Life

Young mind with a big dream

Thinks of the future

Flowing in reality

Water for all

To sustain Uganda

Safe water and sanitation;

Taking actions

To effect a positive change

Not just for one

But for all the creatures

Who thirst for many decades.

fountain of dreams

somehow, dreams dwell

in the sun, the moon

 and the stars,

this time, i stand

beside a fountain

to wish not;

but to discern

the mirrors of the clear blue sky,

& life's enormous blessings.

Ambushed

trapped.

in a quagmire of enmity

and kvetching aubade

at the concealing stilts

of unfounded cults

of clashing blackholes

of dying breathes

of the unforeseen

black and white.

Swapna
Behera

Swapna Behera is a trilingual poet, translator, environmentalist, editor from India and author of seven books of different genres including one on children's literature on Environment. She is the recipient of International UGADI AWARD 2019, honoured from Gujurat Sahitya Akademi 2022, 2021 International Poesis Award of Honor as Jury, Pentasi B World Fellow Poet, Honoured Poet of India from Seychelles Government and International awards from Algeria, Morocco, Kajhakhstan, modern Arabic Literary Renaissance of Egypt, International Arts Council Argentina etc. Her stories, poems, articles are published in many International and National magazines and ezines. Her poem A NIGHT IN THE REFUGEE CAMP is translated into 67 languages. She has received over 60 National and International Awards. At present she is the Cultural Ambassador for India and South Asia of Inner Child and the life member of Odisha Environmental Society

Email
swapna.behera@gmail.com

Web Site
http://swapnabehera.in/

Everything is well if there is a Well

a six-year-old boy
grade one student
 understands the devastation
Water, water, water the basic need
no clean water to drink
so people die
Says Ryan Hreljac
the founder of Ryan Well foundation
to educate children
about sanitation and safe water
to improve the lives of Vulnerable people
a life saver he is
seventeen countries across the globe
have supported his project
when he was in primary school in Uganda
he raised money, did household work
 for his community, got the inspiration
from his teacher Mrs Prest
Ryan at the age of nineteen
 became a compelling voice
 to think about pure water for the people
he is a crisis manager and a change maker
recipient of many awards
"World is like a great big puzzle
and we have to figure out where our pieces fit"
says he
"for me it is water, clean water for all to drink"
he started speaking in clubs
classes and raised fund
His Ugandan pen pal Jimmy
is his inspiration of WASH project
the motto of WASH is

water, sanitation and hygiene
awareness of community
to take responsibility
a grade one student thought
clean water is every one's right
the boy taught a lesson
isn't he a great teacher?
standing ovation to this child
well done, Ryan
everything is well if there is a well near by
everything is well if each one gets pure water

a dozen of red bangles

when I was a child
I used to wait for the bangle seller
who comes to the lane each week
my mother buys colourful bangles
how I wish to have red bangles
my mother said
"This is not the time for putting on bangles
you are only five years"
I with zoomed eyes
wait with patience to grow
and have these luxurious red bangles
I asked mama "Is it too expensive?"
she says "no, but you are too young
bangles are not for tiny girls
concentrate on studies."

when I became a teenager
again, the desire popped up
red bangles with golden lines flashed
but the answer came so quickly
this time my elder sister said
"Good girls can have red bangles during marriage time
and certainly not before"

when I got married, I had plenty of bangles
with all colours of rainbow
but have no liberty to choose
 as someone has all authentic rights
over my life to decide my dress or ornament
red is certainly a childish choice as was told

when I became a granny
again, the red bangles should not be the priority
I was too old, it looks so funny
my grand daughter said

lo behold
 now I am sleeping
with a dozen red bangles in right hand
and another in the left hand
each member remembers my choice
so, I am happy
the only thing is that
I am inside the coffin
neither can I smile nor express my joy
 can not thank you enough
for these red bangles
a whole life passed
to get these precious documents
is liberty achieved or earned?
happiness is so expensive, isn't it ?

if at all …..

if at all I can conceive a forest
I can implant ;
extend my roots to reach you
to be strong
my leaves can give
oxygen to all

if at all I can sing the first anthem
I can submerge all disparities
with love, humility and kindness
I will sing for the war victims

if at all I can write my last poem
my bones will scream the slogan
let there be plants on the deactivated land mines
do not ask me to dance on your rhythm
I am the dance, I am the song

if at all I can create new alphabets
I will dance and sing with
new promises for eternal smile …..

Albert 'Infinite' Carrasco

Albert 'Infinite' Carassco

Albert "Infinite The Poet" Carrasco is an urban poet, mentor and public speaker.

Albert believes his experience of growing up in poverty, dealing with drugs and witnessing murder over and over were lessons learnt, in order to gain knowledge to teach. Albert's harsh reality and honesty is a powerfully packed punch delivered through rhyme. Infinite grew up in the east part of the Bronx and still resides there, so he knows many young men will follow the same dark path he followed looking for change. The life of crime should never be an option to being poor but it is, very often.

Infinite poetry @lulu.com

Alcarrasco2 on YouTube

Infinite the poet on reverbnation

Infinite Poetry

http://www.lulu.com/us/en/shop/al-infinite-carrasco/infinite-poetry/paperback/product-21040240.html

Ryan Hreljac

My first grade teacher, Mrs. Prest explained to my class that there were Kids around the world sick and dying because they didn't have clean water.

That touched my soul and I was just six year's old. I thought every kid lived as I did.
Happy, joyful and fun times that led to a lot of laughter,
I couldn't understand why there was children just like me somewhere struggling to eat and drink as well as

Finding shelter to protect themselves from high heat, bugs and rainy weather.
Immediately I had visions of helping those poor children, that was my plan,
one way or another i was going to lend a helping hand. I did chores for cash,

Hoping to earn enough money to build a well really fast. Unfortunately seventy
dollars wasn't enough to build a well for fresh water. I wasn't going to give up on
them, that first grade project eventually became Ryan's Well Foundation. My drive
to help as a kid continued through adulthood, I graduated from Halifax in Canada

With a double major in International Development and Political Science. After
College I returned to the foundation as a project manager, now I'm the Executive
Director building wells all over so families can have access to clean water.

Infinite

Hello everyone my name is Infinite! Before it was infinite they called me statistic, that wild puerto rican kid from the south bronx goes ballistic, 5 6 but don't get it twisted, you'll get lifted, besides his Napoleon syndrome, in any hood he's respected as corleon, I say yeah next to diamonds in the rough I'm a Siera Leon! Most drank 40's of ole e, I was straight moet and chandon, wasn't gang banging, we were a bunch of che guevaras, trying to make life more better, threw bombs to my dogs like mike vic, in the boonies in the bricks, our jerseys were guayaberas, turned a nyc housing authority lobby into la perla puerto rico!, with this place if your not familiar, ill just say on vaca this isn't a place I recommend you go. My roots run deep so I planted myself into these new york streets, a few branches sprouted a Whole tree, in a forest unseen. I was a ray of hope to the reys(kings) and (reinas) that couldn't cope, they saw when I came and went, hear none see none, I helped with compra(food shopping) and rent. I know it sounds dark, and wasn't a loan shark, but when there's no stamps or ebt and pockets empty, they didn't mind me lending from what I made in the park. I know some might criticize, by all mean do, I'm not trying to glamorize, nor advertise, that would be disrespectful to the dead men in my crew, my retinas recorded I'm playing it back for you, what I went through, what my crew went through, so maybe some can avoid it. In the hood my names exploited, if there was a hood pope I probably will be anointed, my peoples know I'm an anomaly, moms is christian while dad was god body, moms had me watching david and goliath, while dad made me quote the 1 - 36, and learn what the 7 * (is, I went to a mosque and a church, I was reincarnated two times through mental birth but at the same time, I love rice and beans, I just don't do swine. My thoughts run richly rampant reaching reality's realm of righteous religions, my brain rambunctiously races to revive non evolving radical minds

Preventing Hurt and Pain

I stood behind a hole in a brick wall taking orders, to owning my very own drive thru/walk thru in housing quarters, sometimes the lines circled the corner, sometimes the entire block, had 20's of powder, or 5 or 10 dollar ready rock, had look outs yelling subiendo and bajando, line watchers blowing covers on 5 0, enforcers enforcing cop and go, fuck the world were gonna blow from selling blow, when your at the bottom, to the top is the only place you can go, we were young aristocrats claiming blocks like kids playing with hasbro. Moneys bubbling, the diamonds on gold was blinging. we're hood stars, everywhere we went we had respect like young scars, dudes had hoopties we drove luxury cars, I could spend ten grand a day, on chics and bottles, it didn't matter i was gonna still re up tomorrow. Everything was fine and dandy, mothers and fathers still had their kids, they was a family...that was In the 80's, my young blind decisions along with now dead men's opinions ruined family trees. Drugs and guns took the best from me. Now they're urban legends.. I miss them. I'm back to un weave what was woven. after me, my same path was chosen. A lot of the kids in the 718 or now labeled future 187's, my duty is to intercept them from being incarcerated or murdered and left on the same corner they hustle on leaking out red rum. Im trying to change the game, like removing the baking soda and water out cocaine, to prevent future hurt and pain.

Michelle
Joan
Barulich

Michelle Joan Barulich was born in Honolulu, Hawaii on the island of Oahu. She started writing poetry and songs with her younger brother Paul. They have written many songs in their teen years. She is currently studying Alternative Medicine and would like to become a Homeopathic Doctor. Michelle loves all kinds of animals and birds; she does wild rehabilitation. She has also rescued rock pigeons that make great pets.

https://www.facebook.com/michelle.barulich

Ryan's Well

Flowing, clean water

For all who thirsts

Thank you for helping the poor.

Your passion is honored.

Your vision is inspiring.

Let the water of life

continue to flow...

The Silent Wind

Where I used to know where I wanted to go
And where I used to know where I wanted to roam
The news came on a sunny day
and that's where it all seems to end
Now, tell me where do I begin?
What do I do with my life now?
What do I do? and where do I go?
Can't seem to picture your love has gone away
I can feel the pain in my heart and mind
Can't seem to shake it off
I wear the mask you have sewn together for me, for me
And where I used to know where I wanted to roam
Run, run with the silent wind behind me
Can't escape to another world
Can't seem to find death when I seek it
The hours seem so long
The nights are darker then hell
I walk into the distant hall
Where the candles burn for you, for me
The softness of the music
Takes me to you in another time world
And where I used to know where I wanted to go
And where I used to know where I wanted to roam...

Away Unto Me

The light has a secret behind its force
Pictures of life know the meaning
And the flame of the fire knows how to throw you off
The moon lit with caution
And every cry you know is heard
And every tear is counted
And every different road we take will become as one in the
end
Away unto me
I love
Away unto me
I hate
Away unto me
I wish
The magic of the unicorn
Will steal our hearts
And children will be wise until the end
My hope is like a dream
My dream is something I want to be
The words play an emotion
With every line there's a feelin
Away unto me
I love
Away unto me
I hate
Away unto me
I wish
Images reflect in space
A time I see you
Nine years ago in the past
Away unto me
Away unto you
Away unto me and you...

Eliza Segiet

Eliza Segiet graduated with a Master's Degree in Philosophy at Jagiellonian University.
Received *Global Literature Guardian Award* – from Motivational Strips, World Nations

Writers' Union and Union Hispanomundial De Escritores (UHE) 2018.

Nominated for the Pushcart Prize 2019, 2021.

Laureate *Naji Naaman Literary Prize 2020, International Award Paragon of Hope* (2020),

World Award 2020 *Cesar Vallejo* for Literary Excellence.

Laureate of the Special Jury *Sahitto International Award* 2021, World Award *Premiul Fănuş Neagu* 2021.

Finalist *Golden Aster Book* World Literary Prize 2020, *Mili Dueli* 2022, Voci nel deserto 2022.

At the international Festival of Poetry CAMPIONATO MONDIALE DI POESIA (2021/2022) she won the title of vice-champion of the world.

Award BHARAT RATNA RABINDRANATH TAGORE INTERNATIONAL AWARD (2022).

The Land
To Ryan Hreljacow

When he was seven years old,
he learnt
that somewhere far,
in a place
he had not heard about,
was a waterless land.
–The lack of it,
which did not let others live,
made him want to act.
He started to collect money
to help the parched ones.

Now he is happy
with what he has made.
Those with dried-out mouths before
now get
their blood of life from the wells
he's been building for years.

He's succeeded in what he was dreaming of!
He's harnessed something
that seemed unharnessable.

Translated by Dorota Stępińska

Triad

Between the multifoliate branches
– only for the descendants –
a hidden triad
of sculpted words:

please,
thank you,
sorry.

Every day we see emoticons.
Hearts, flowers
and lack of understanding.

A monitor screen
becomes the real world
of homo sapiens.

Translated by Artur Komoter

Scratches

Wishing to gain trust,
they take on artificial faces,
mythical reality
allows to survive.

However, after a while
we see that
plastic people
no longer delight

– they have scratches.

Translated by Artur Komoter

William
S.
Peters Sr.

Bill's writing career spans a period of over 50 years. Being first Published in 1972, Bill has since went on to Author in excess of 50 additional Volumes of Poetry, Short Stories, etc., expressing his thoughts on matters of the Heart, Spirit, Consciousness and Humanity. His primary focus is that of Love, Peace and Understanding!

Bill says . . .

I have always likened Life to that of a Garden. So, for me, Life is simply about the Seeds we Sow and Nourish. All things we "Think and Do", will "Be" Cause and eventually manifest itself to being an "Effect" within our own personal "Existences" and "Experiences" . . . whether it be Fruit, Flowers, Weeds or Barren Landscapes! Bill highly regards the Fruits of his Labor and wishes that everyone would thus go on to plant "Lovely" Seeds on "Good Ground" in their own Gardens of Life!

to connect with Bill, he is all things Inner Child

www.iaminnerchild.com

Personal Web Site

www.iamjustbill.com

Water . . . Sacred

I thirst, I thirst,
But let it be no more,
For it is not fair,
But who cares?

The river is far away,
And all the dirty, muddy waters
Have just about dried up

Who will hear our plea O world,
Who amongst you all
Will hear our call
To life, for life

Dig me a well . . . please

Water is sacred,
Don't you know?

Ryan Hreljac came,
He saw,
He conquered,
But he can not do it all alone

He heard our plea
To be free
Of yet another choke-hold,
Another burden
That circumstance
Has placed upon us
And more to come
If we do nothing
Won't you help, won't you hear the plea?

Water . . . Sacred

Letting

The great 'letting'
Is upon us ....
.....
We hold on to things
That are better to be
Let go,
As we let go things
We should hold tight to

There are people and places,
Things and times,
Memories and moments
Whose values
Are unfathomable
At the very least

Who amongst us
Can assess with certainty
The value of one's experientialness?

We blindly attempt
To navigate our lives
Only to
At some time understand
That all things
Have meaning ...
The good, the bad
And the obscure and ambiguous

Life is like a tour
Where wonders,

Small and large
And in-between
Are presented to us
To ingest, and/or digest,
While the test of life
Is always being administered
.....
The Proctors
Are ever prevalent,
So sharpen your pencils
And let the letting begin

Voice

Across the seas
Within the canyons,
Upon the meadows
Wandering in the Forrest,
Dancing on the winds
Reaching for the Sun
Wrestling with the storms
Painting and sculpting the clouds,
Running with the streams,
Be it but liquid consciousness,
Or liquid and consciousness ...
There is a omnipresent voice
Omniscient and Omnipotent
That is indwelling in my
Private Omniverse

It speaks to me
And I to it
As we reflect one
And another's countenance
Upon the face
Of the waters of existence

The Water Bearer is with us
Letting loose the spirit
Upon the Earth ....
I know its soul,
And it knows mine.

'The Voice' speaks....
Listen

The Butterfly Effect

"IS" in effect

June

2023

Featured Poets

~ * ~

Kay Peters

Carthornia Kouroupos

Andrew Kouroupos

Faleeha Hassan

i Fly

because I Can

... said the Dreamer to the world.

www.iamjustbill.com

112

Kay
Peters

Kay Peters is a registered nurse, and a retired Oncology Clinical Nurse Specialist. Her poems have appeared in *Philadelphia Poets, Schuylkill Valley Journal. US 1 Worksheets, More Challenges for the Delusional and Philadelphia Stories*

Black Snake

Last summer, at our first encounter it slipped away
smooth as black ribbon in the wind.

It lives in our woods, its den the tangle of branches
scattered on the bank above the stream

Later when our paths crossed, it raised
its head, turned its dark glass eyes toward me

Then glided toward the stream,
shaping Ss in summer dust.

It hibernates now with others
coiled in a mass to survive the cold.

If it returns with spring and I do not care
for its company, it will be I who must slip away.

The Soldier's Child (World War II)

More frightened
by cartoon ants
with slanted eyes
and bristle-faced foxes
wearing swastikas
than pictures of planes
with painted suns
falling from flaming skies
or black-booted men
marching
through ash and smoke—
the child was told:
Help your mother.
You must be good.
Pray for your father
to come home.
The child prayed—
Daddy, Please come home.

Hearts

She considers the dimensions
of hearts — the giant red heart
at the Franklin Institute
smelling like a musty classroom
its recorded lub-dupp lub-dupp
resonates in fiberglass walls
schools of children swarm up and down
its narrow steps their calls echo
through its chambers.

Her heart she knows is the size
of her fist smooth and slippery
should one care to grasp it
at night she sometimes hears
its soft lub-dupp lub-dupp
whispering as cardiac muscle
fibers contract and relax
bicuspid and tricuspid
valves open and close
rhythmic, measured, predictable.

Carthornia
Kouroupos

Carthornia Kouroupos was born and raised in Brooklyn, New York. She currently lives in South Jersey with the husband and children. She is an English Professor at Rowan College South Jersey and has an M.A. in the Writing Arts from Rowan University. She writes children's stories, essays, poetry, fiction, and nonfiction.

Carthornia can be contacted at: ckouroupos@verizon.net

Brother Where Art Thou?

December 1981. The operation was swift,
Preformed with precision and skill,
It was as quick as the knock on the door,
I answered it.
No organs were left out of place,
The job was done so well.
I was told you were no more,
Gone,
Not to be found in the tiniest places,
Or even in foreign lands.
My heart turned to lead and dragged me to my knees,
As my red hot liquid turned into small beads of ice cold clots,
That forced the river from my soul so deep,
So deep,
It took many years to crest,
Before I could rest,
My tattered being,
So broken, damaged, wrecked.
Didn't know how to pick up the pieces of what was left.
I wanted to come to the place,
Where you're final home was made,
You laid there losing warmth,
Until you glowed with an unfamiliar look.
I never did, though…I was afraid,
Afraid I'd find you,
Afraid of what you'd say.
I just waited for you to come to me,
And you did that very first night.
I was happy,
And surprised.
You told me it wasn't true,

That they had not done that to you,
That you had gone away,
Your absence a delay,
Until you were forgotten by those who would lay you
down,
In a hole,
Six feet underground.
I was so happy to see you, well,
And proclaimed my love for you,
And as I rose with the sun,
The truth pulled back the veil,
The operation *had* made a change,
So deep within my heart,
That when awake I dream you dead,
And when asleep, alive.

Funhouse

There is a "funhouse" inside of me,

with a maze of mirrors exposing the threads in my seams,

alterations pushing to get out.

I stare,

in the mirrors—

waiting for insight.

But,

insight doesn't come,

I continue to wait,

as my alterations increase in size,

breaking through the blood stained threads.

Stolen Poems

Poets lifting my words,

Showing my story telling my plight,

Manifestations of my life laid out in plan site,

I should have locked my thoughts,

So they couldn't have drop from my ears,

So many words,

so loud,

So loud,

My words have been lifted,

And laid down on the white spaces of others,

Who claim the fame.

Carthornia Kouroupos

Andy
Kouroupos

Andrew Kouroupos was born and raised in Brooklyn, New York. He currently lives in New Jersey with his wife and children . He writes children's stories, essays, poetry, fiction, and nonfiction. He is also a screenwriter whose screenplay was presented at the Sundance Film Festival.

Andrew can be contacted at: akouroupos@verizon.net

Dead Poets Society

Bleed us lest our egos bruise

from droughts of praise and rave reviews,

though fleeting is our verse that shows

a flair that sheds our emperor's clothes.

Bleed us and exact our flesh

each drop and pound for words afresh,

as ransom though our voices die

in no name graves where poets lie.

Summer Rain

We met without an invitation

which never stopped you, nonetheless.

A patter on the hospital window,

was why I asked you to come in.

You stayed outside performing,

a tango on my sick room glass,

entreating me to brave the raindrops,

and join you in your summer dance.

A View from the Wall

A monolith I loom over wounds unhealed,
as Cain did to Abel, I'm he unconcealed.
Four hundred miles of a prison austere,
a bastion of hate standing year after year.

Entrenched in the soil I rise heavenly bound,
my shadow on Canaan casts on hell on the ground.
I'm snaked across village and field commandeered,
apartheid of kin for the kindred that's feared.

Injustice I've seen from the back of my stead,
spawning blows that are struck from the justice not spread.
In courtrooms of might citing ancient of days,
claiming browner of skin have no rights to appraise.

Through West Bank to Rafat to home of the manger,
I burden the yolks of the natives now strangers.
My slabs with barbed crowns piercing spirits and veins,
turning dreams dripping red and their freedom to chains.

Stand, I do not without eyes and pricked ears.
Feel, I cannot without conscience and tears.
I am the Wall who saw Zion succumb,
to the beasts of their past and the beast they've become.

Faleeha Hassan

Faleeha Hassan is a poet, teacher, editor, writer, playwriter from Iraq, who now lives in the USA. She is the first woman wrote poetry for children in Iraq. She received master's degree in Arabic literature, and published (25) books. Her poems have been translated into (20) languages, her book nominated to Pulitzer Prize on 2018, and PushCaret Prize 2019; Winer of the Women of Excellence Inspiration award from SJ magazine 2020; Winer of Grand Jury Award (the Sahitto International Award for Literature 2021); One of the Women of Excellence selection committee 2023.

Ms. Hassan is the Inner Child Cultural Ambassador for Iraq, USA

Email : d.fh88@yahoo.com

Faleeha Hassan

Hypnotizing an Iraqi child

Uh my baby
As soon as you reach the age of eighteen,
you will be in an eddy of the adversity
even if you turn into a scarecrow,
no matter how hard you try
you will not be able to frighten a warplane heading towards
you,
that moment you will remember your home that the bomb
joked with,
then dispersed it in flaming shards.
You may remember your life,
that once the warning sirens screamed turned
into a very valuable piece that death needed
so badly to complete its collection.
You may pray
but your voice will be stuck in the shape of your words,
try to smile but you remain completely
 unable to mitigate the devastation that sweeping you down.
In the war only the skulls will remain calm,
opening their mouths to the end,
please, please
don't grow
sleep tight

Snow and Smoke Song

Before you bought her a flower, you should have expected
that,
It's snowing
I'm watching you now
Freezing together
You and her leaves
Maybe your girl now
Her mouth flirts with a warmth of cappuccino mug
Her body drowning in the folds of a woolen robe
But you
The closing doors stare at the stupidity of your t-shirt
Shaking their heads
Just a tree bending to the wind
Begging it to be affectionate tonight
Not to hurt your bones
Like it did with her branches
Don't worry
 Everyone make mistakes
He did too
He ignored my advice when I said:
Kiss the paper and send it to me
The kiss is more affectionate than words
If you intend to write me a love letter,
The years are passing by
Planets are fading away
And the earth is shrinking from its edges
However
I haven't seen yet the shadow of the postman's car.

My Fault

Uh, I 'v forgot it –

the war that has just passed away two moments

Yes, two moments

I forgot to throw stones behind it - as my mom said -

So, it's returned back

With all its death

And

will swallow all of us again.

Remembering

our fallen soldiers of verse

Janet Perkins Caldwell

February 14, 1959 ~ September 20, 2016

Alan W. Jankowski

16 March 1961 ~ 10 March 2017

Inner Child Press

News

Published Books

by

Poetry Posse Members

We are so excited to share and announce a few of the current books, as well as the new and upcoming books of some of our Poetry Posse authors.

On the following pages we present to you ...

Alicja Maria Kuberska

Jackie Davis Allen

Gail Weston Shazor

hülya n. yılmaz

Nizar Sartawi

Elizabeth E. Castillo

Faleeha Hassan

Fahredin Shehu

Kimberly Burnham

Caroline 'Ceri' Nazareno

Eliza Segiet

Teresa E. Gallion

William S. Peters, Sr.

Now Available

www.innerchildpress.com

Once upon a Time

in

Turkey

hülya n. yılmaz

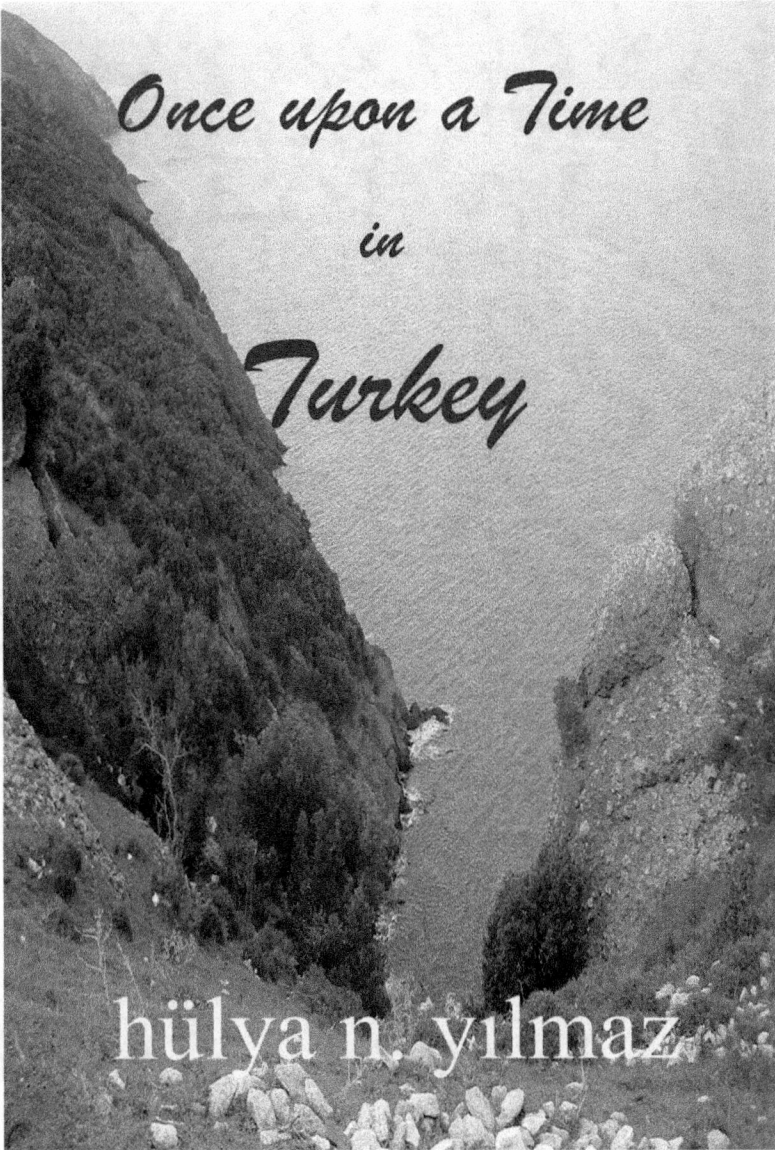

Now Available
www.innerchildpress.com

Unapologetically

BLACK

&

Blues

william s. peters, sr.

Now Available

www.innerchildpress.com

Pulling Coats

Shareef Abdur-Rasheed

Now Available
www.innerchildpress.com

Now Available

www.innerchildpress.com

After the Frost

Alicja Maria Kuberska

Now Available

www.innerchildpress.com

Fahredin Shehu

ORMUS

Now Available

www.innerchildpress.com

Ahead of My Time

. . . from the Streets to the Stages

Albert 'Infinite' Carrasco

Now Available
www.innerchildpress.com

Eliza Segiet

To Be More

www.amazon.com/gp/product/B08MYL5B7S/ref=
dbs_a_def_rwt_hsch_vapi_tkin_p1_i2

Now Available at
www.innerchildpress.com

Scent of Love

Poetry by

Teresa E. Gallion

Now Available

www.innerchildpress.com

Inner Reflections
of the
Muse

Elizabeth Castillo

Now Available

www.innerchildpress.com

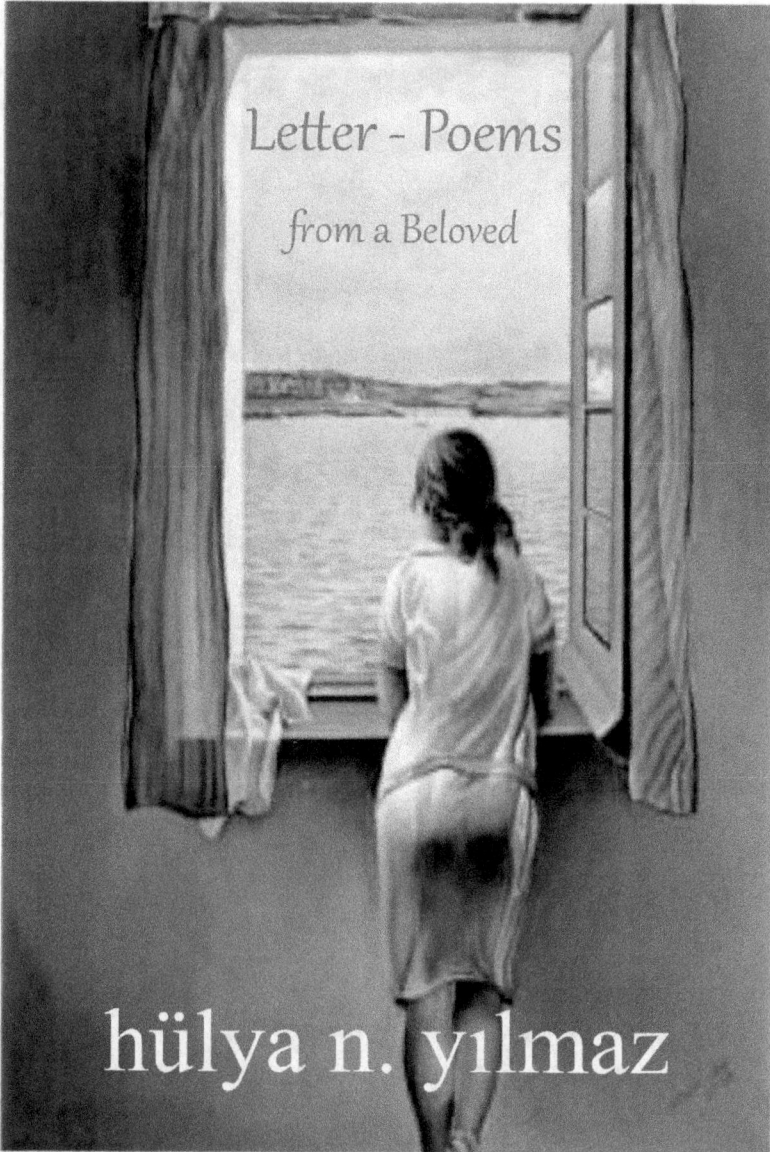

Letter - Poems

from a Beloved

hülya n. yılmaz

Now Available

www.innerchildpress.com

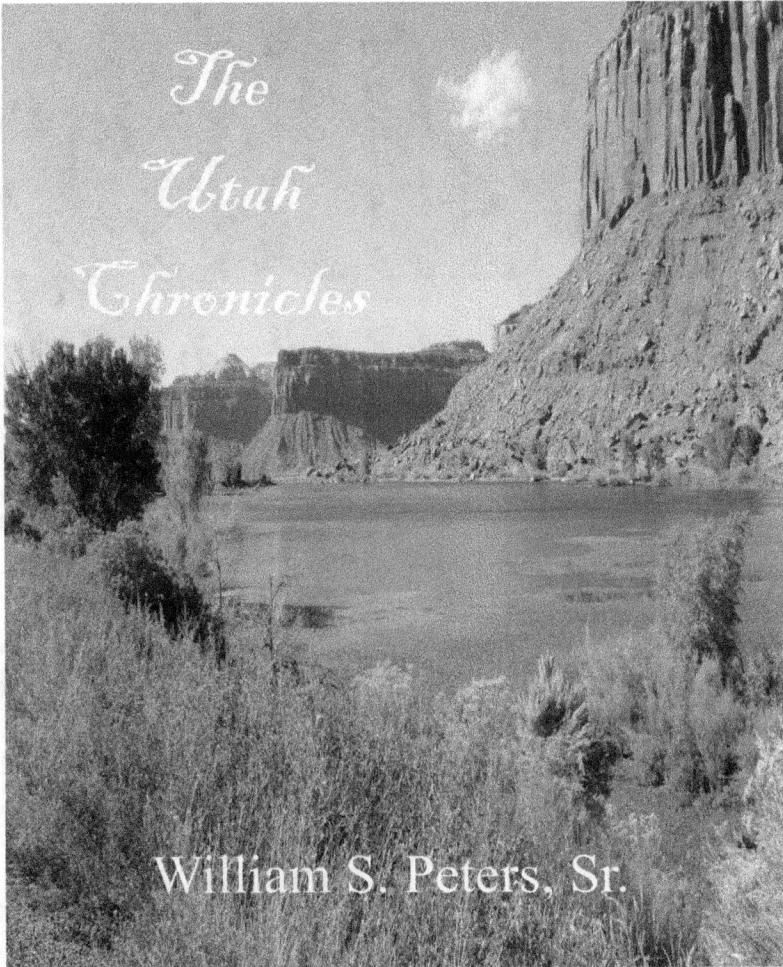

The
Utah
Chronicles

William S. Peters, Sr.

Now Available

www.innerchildpress.com

One Eye Open

u n i r 1.

william s. peters, sr

Now Available
www.innerchildpress.com

The Book of krisar

volume v

william s. peters, sr.

Now Available

www.innerchildpress.com

The Book of krisar

Volume I

william s. peters, sr.

The Book of krisar

Volume II

william s. peters, sr.

Now Available
www.innerchildpress.com

The Book of krisar

Volume III

william s. peters, sr.

The Book of krisar

Volume IV

william s. peters, sr.

Now Available

www.innerchildpress.com

Velvet Passions

of

Calibrated Quarks

Caroline Nazareno-Gabis

Now Available

www.innerchildpress.com

Unpaired

Eliza Segiet

Translated by Artur Komoter

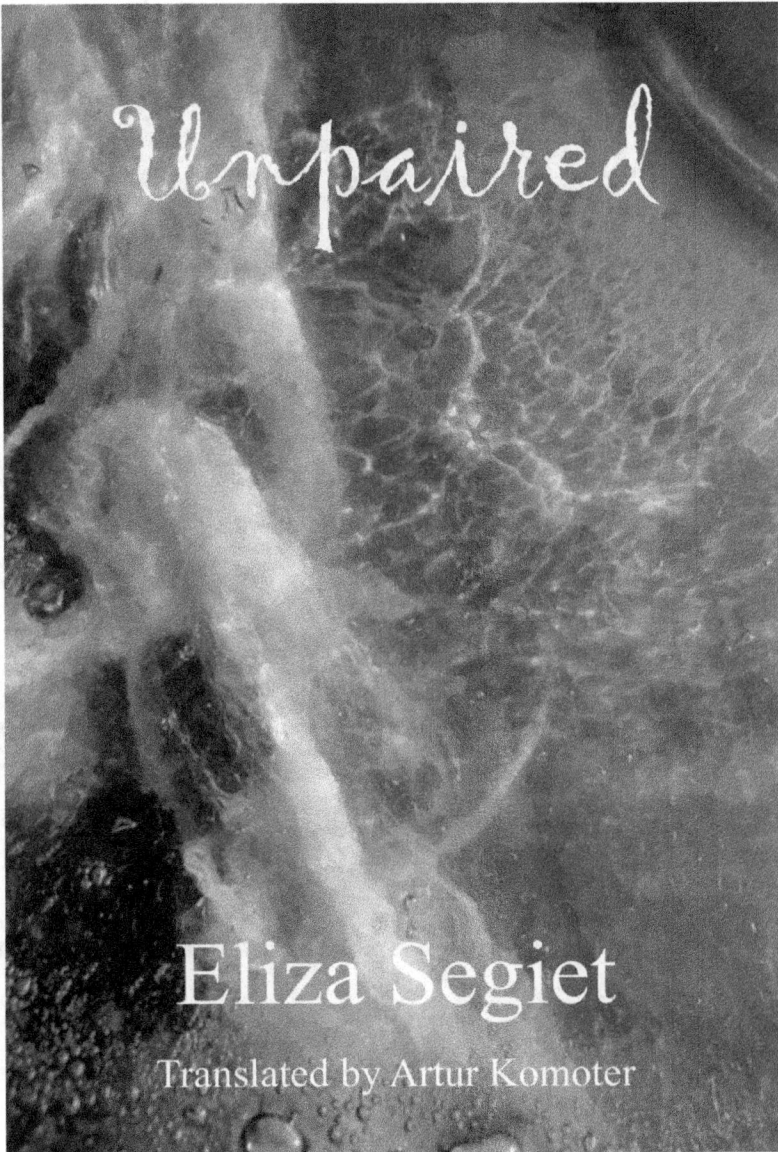

Private Issue

www.innerchildpress.com

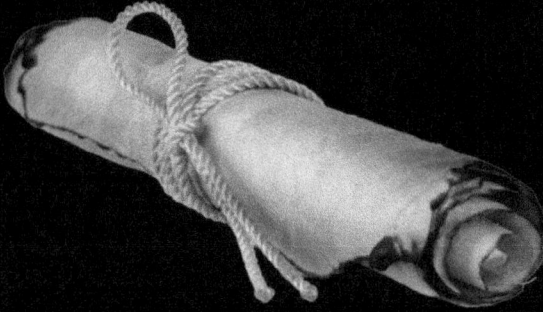

Canlarım
My Lifeblood

poetry in Turkish and English

hülya n. yılmaz

Now Available
www.innerchildpress.com

Butterfly's Voice

Faleeha Hassan

Translated by William M. Hutchins

Now Available at

www.innerchildpress.com

No Illusions

Through the Looking Glass

Jackie Davis Allen

Now Available at

www.innerchildpress.com

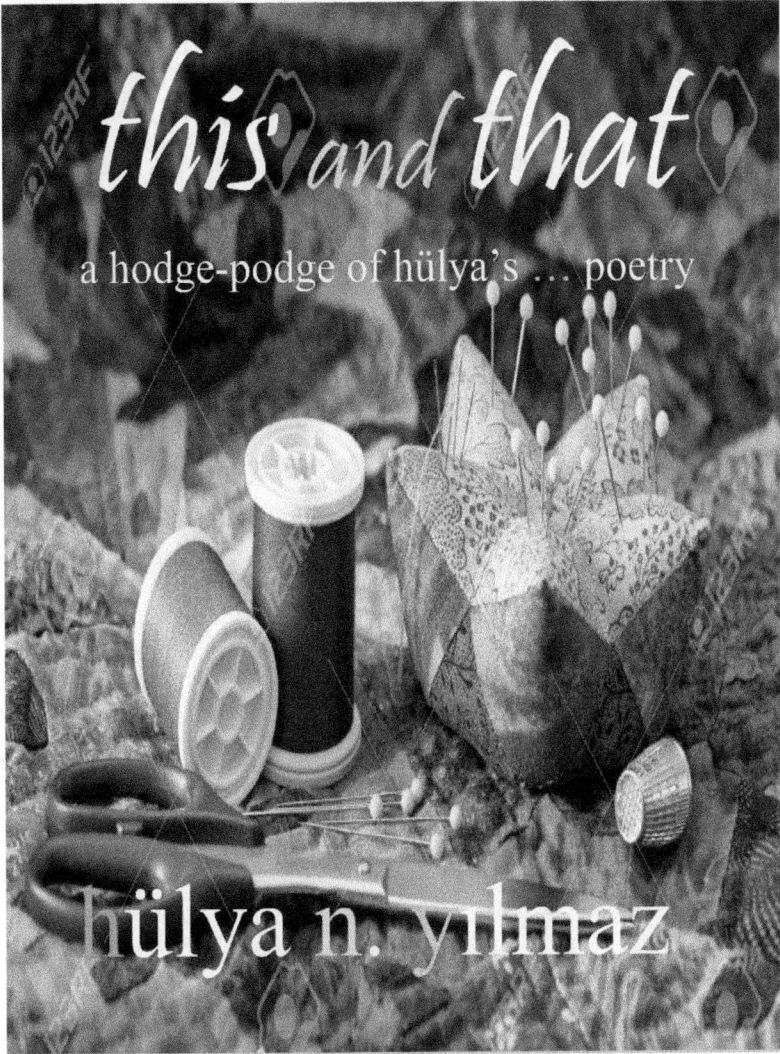

this and that

a hodge-podge of hülya's ... poetry

hülya n. yılmaz

Now Available at

www.innerchildpress.com

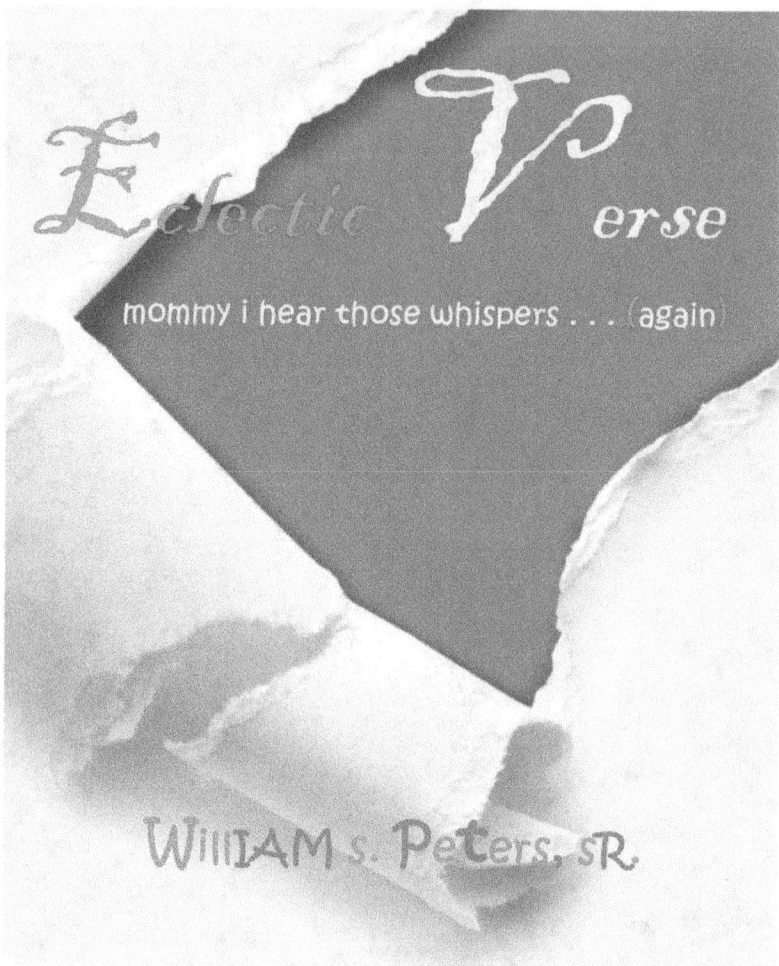

Now Available at

www.innerchildpress.com

HERENOW

FAHREDIN SHEHU

Now Available at
www.innerchildpress.com

Magnetic People

Eliza Segiet

Translated by Artur Komoter

Now Available at
www.innerchildpress.com

Dark Side
of the
Moon

Jackie Davis Allen

Now Available at
www.innerchildpress.com

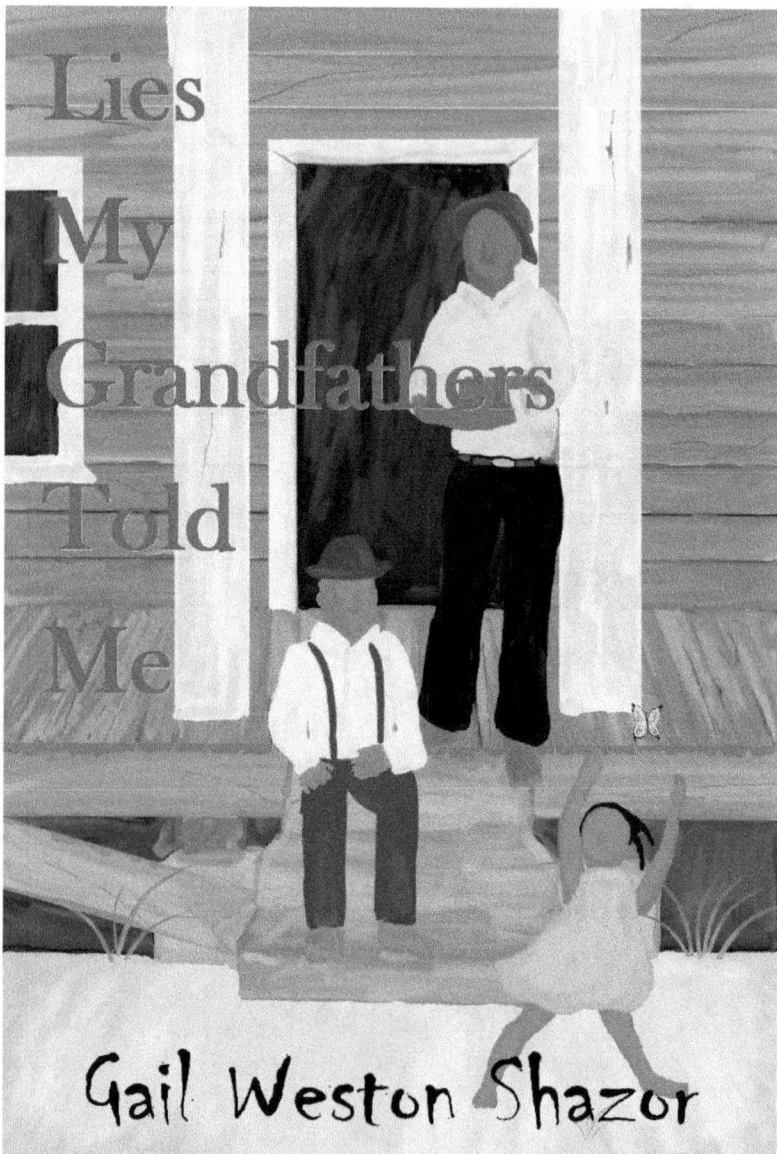

Lies My Grandfathers Told Me

Gail Weston Shazor

Now Available at
www.innerchildpress.com

Aflame

Memoirs in Verse

hülya n. yılmaz

Now Available at
www.innerchildpress.com

Mass Graves

Faleeha Hassan

Now Available at

www.innerchildpress.com

172

Breakfast
for
Butterflies

Faleeha Hassan

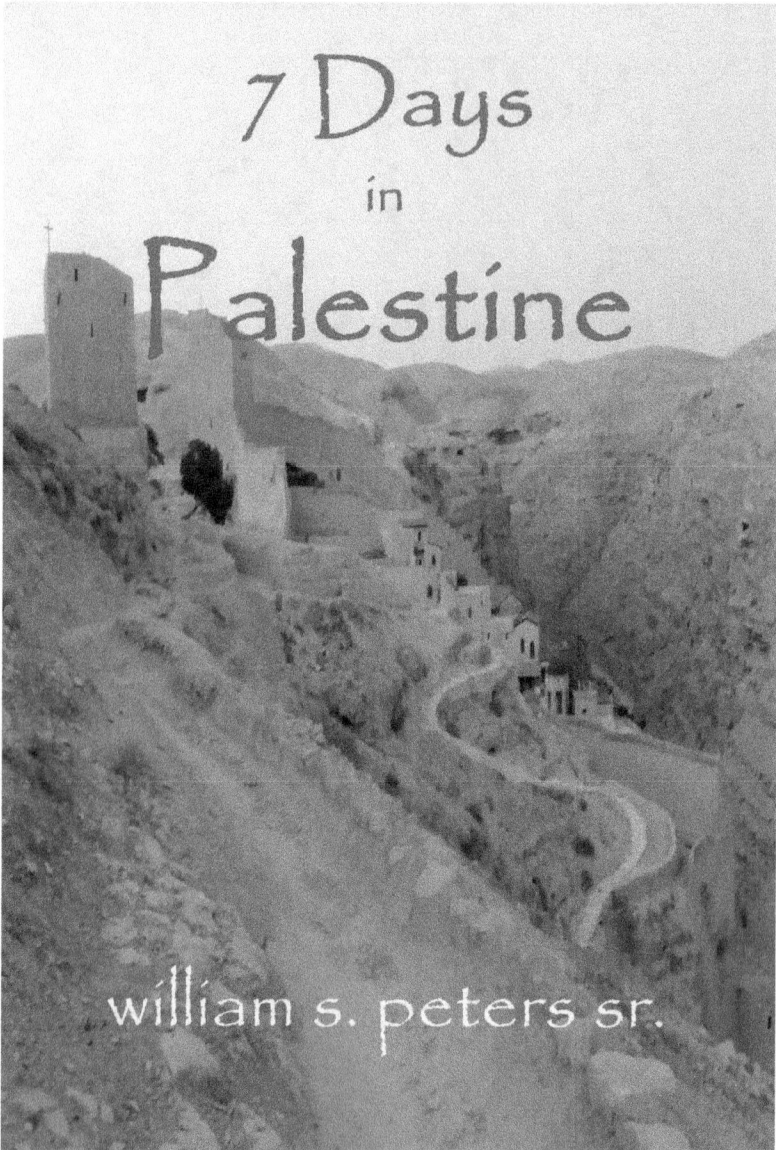

7 Days
in
Palestine

william s. peters sr.

Now Available at
www.innerchildpress.com

inner child press
presents

Tunisian Dreams

william s. peters, sr.

Now Available at
www.innerchildpress.com

INNER CHILD PRESS

THIS IS WHY I
SLEEP

william s. peters sr.

Now Available at
www.innerchildpress.com

Other

Anthological

works from

Inner Child Press International

www.innerchildpress.com

World Healing
World Peace
2022

Poets for Humanity

Now Available

www.worldhealingworldpeacepoetry.com

World Healing World Peace
2020

Poets for Humanity

Now Available

www.worldhealingworldpeacepoetry.com

I want to

LiVe

*an **examination** of Black & White issues*

POETRY

ANALYSES

STORIES

CREATIVE WRITING

CRITICAL ESSAYS

WRITERS FOR HUMANITY

Now Available

www.innerchildpress.com

Inner Child Press International
&
The Year of the Poet
present

Poetry

the best of 2020

Poets of the World

Now Available
www.innerchildpress.com

Inner Child Press International

presents

W.A.R.

We Are Revolution

Poets for Humanity

Now Available
www.innerchildpress.com

the Heart of a Poet

words for a better tomorrow

The Conscious Poets

Now Available
www.innerchildpress.com

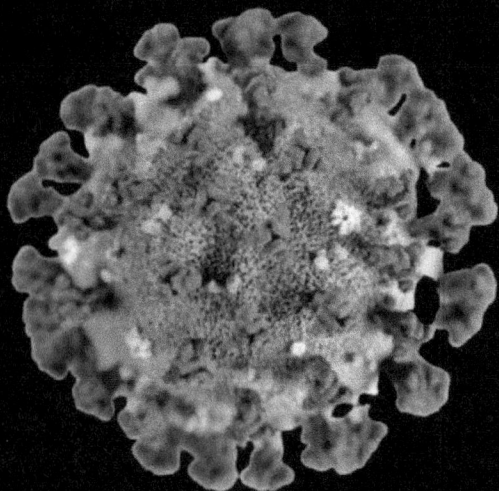

Corona

Social Distancing

Poets for Humanity

Now Available
www.innerchildpress.com

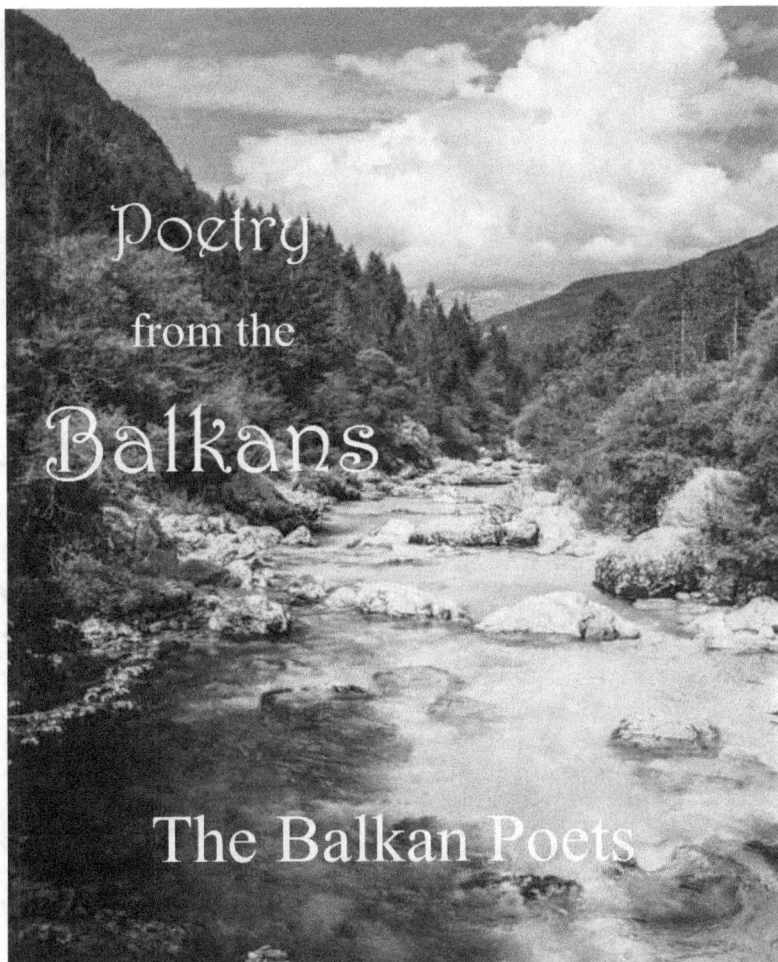

Poetry
from the
Balkans

The Balkan Poets

Now Available at
www.innerchildpress.com

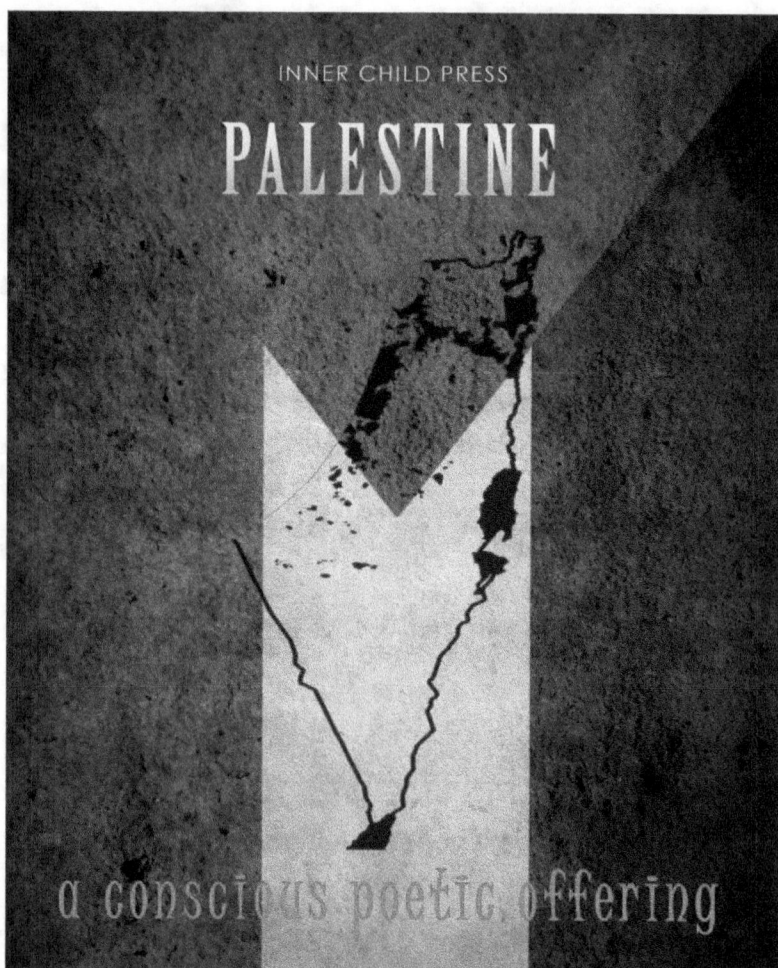

INNER CHILD PRESS

PALESTINE

a conscious poetic offering

Now Available at
www.innerchildpress.com

Now Available at

www.innerchildpress.com

Inner Child Press International
presents

A Love Anthology
2019

The Love Poets

Now Available
www.worldhealingworldpeacepoetry.com

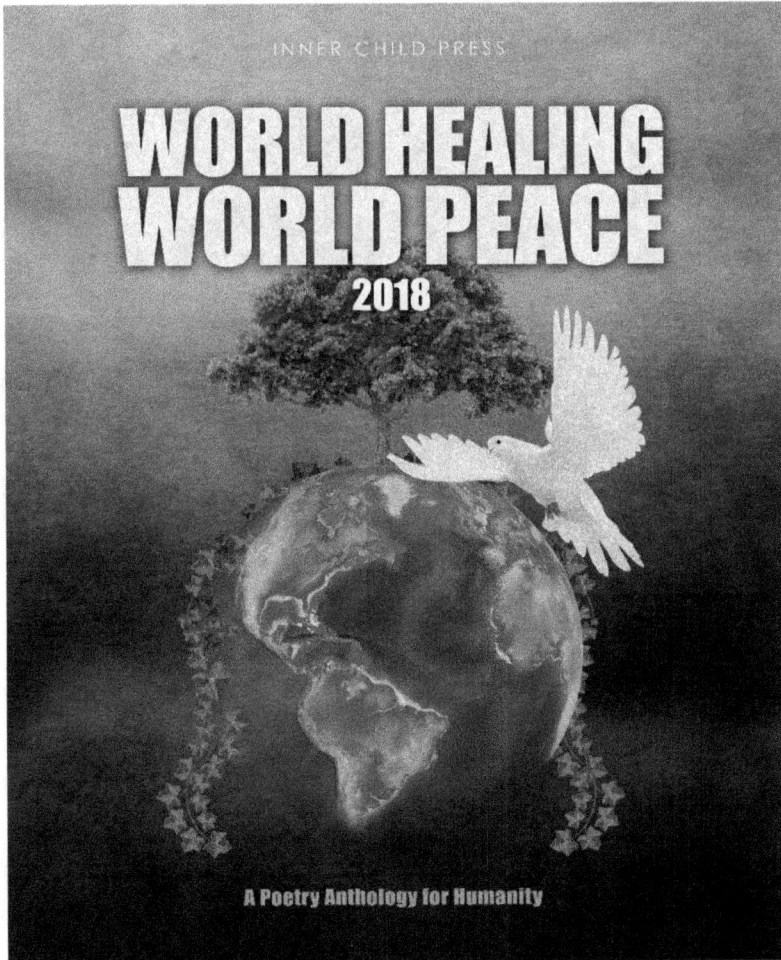

INNER CHILD PRESS

WORLD HEALING WORLD PEACE

2018

A Poetry Anthology for Humanity

Now Available

www.worldhealingworldpeacepoetry.com

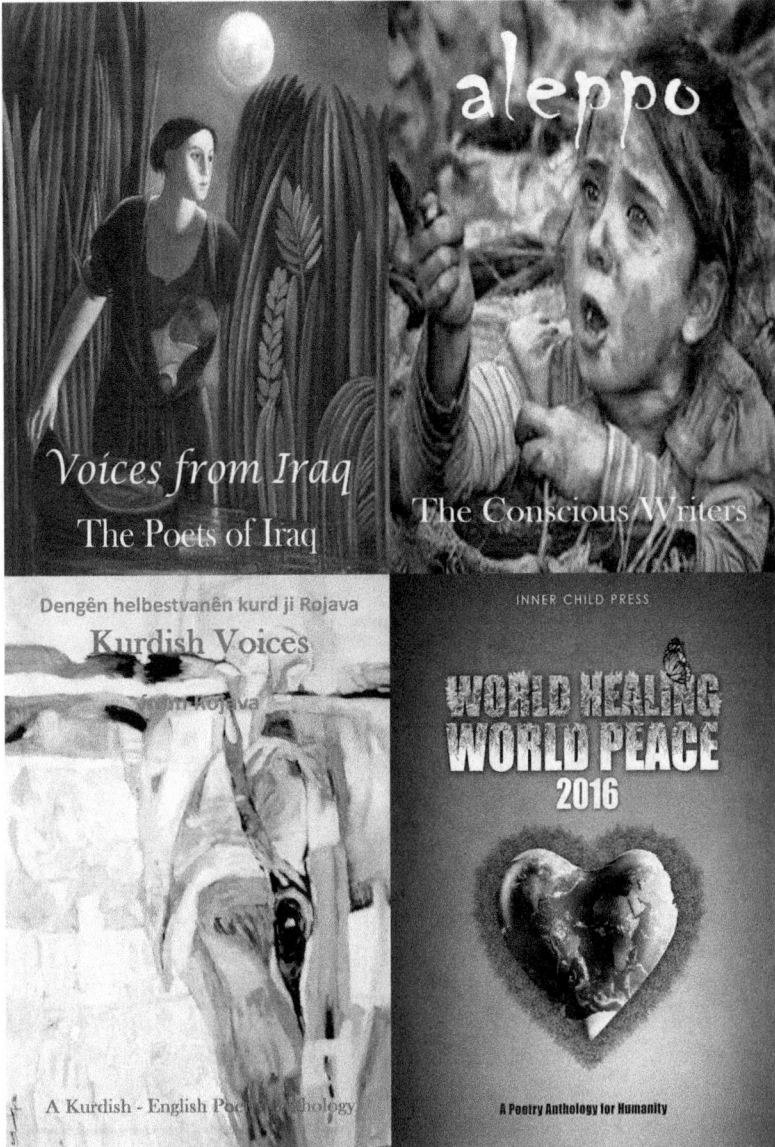

Now Available

www.innerchildpress.com/anthologies

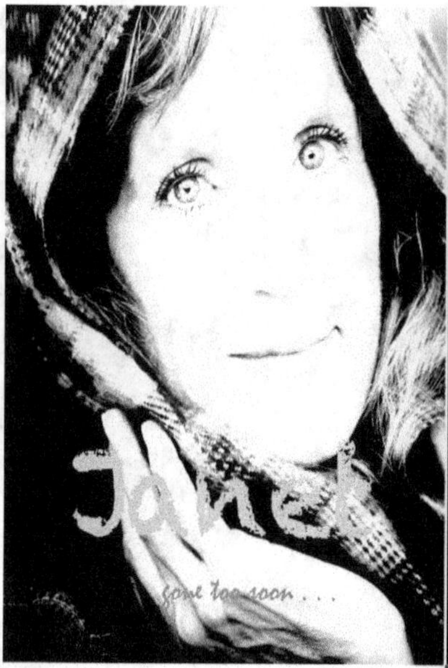

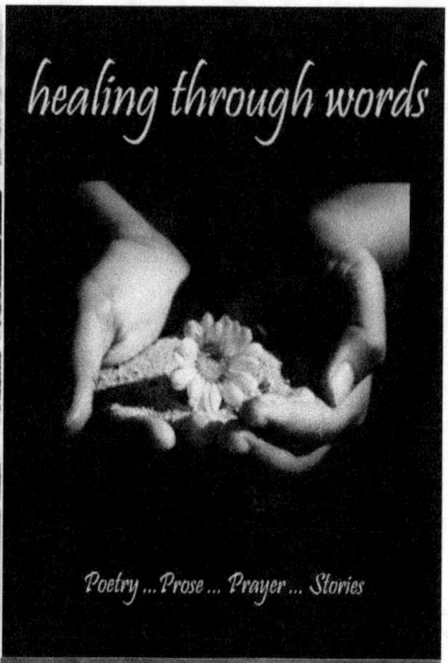

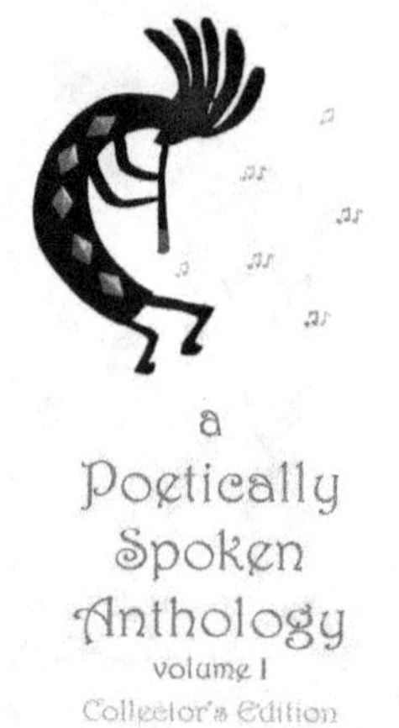

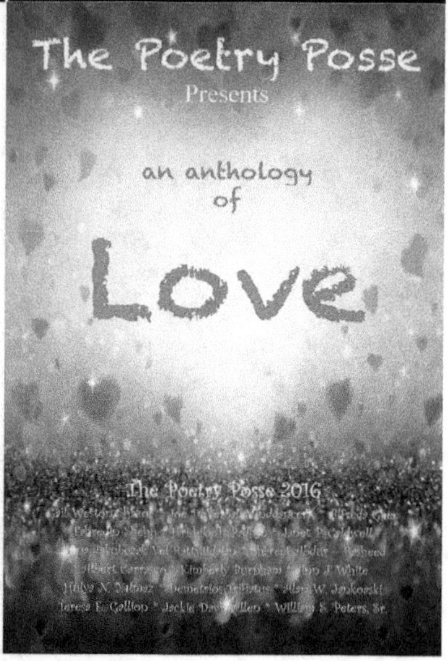

Now Available

www.innerchildpress.com/anthologies

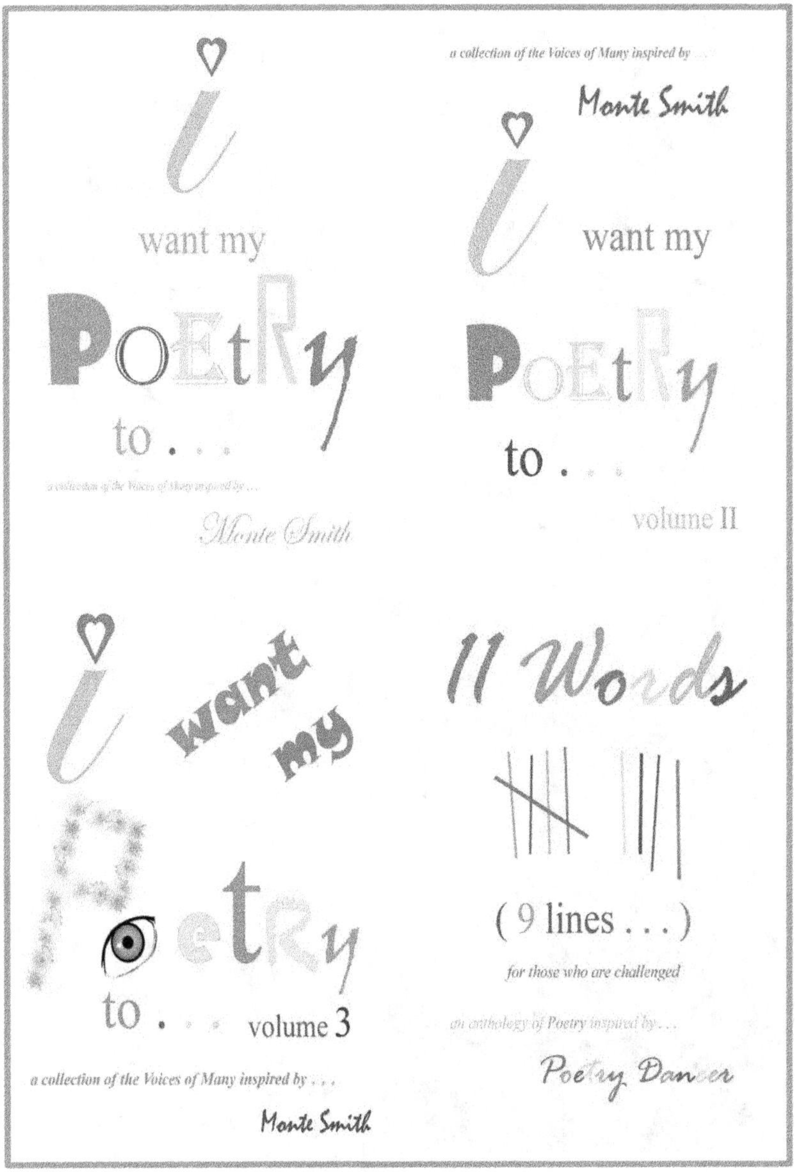

Now Available

www.innerchildpress.com/anthologies

The Year of the Poet
January 2014

The Poetry Posse

Jamie Bond
Gail Weston Shazor
Albert 'Infinite' Carrasco
Siddartha Beth Pierce
Janet P. Caldwell
June 'Bugg' Barefield
Debbie M. Allen
Tony Henninger
Joe DaVerbal Minddancer
Robert Gibbons
Neetu Wali
Shareef Abdur-Rasheed
William S. Peters, Sr.

Carnation

Our January Feature
Terri L. Johnson

the Year of the Poet
February 2014

violets

The Poetry Posse

Jamie Bond
Gail Weston Shazor
Albert 'Infinite' Carrasco
Siddartha Beth Pierce
Janet P. Caldwell
June 'Bugg' Barefield
Debbie M. Allen
Tony Henninger
Joe DaVerbal Minddancer
Robert Gibbons
Neetu Wali
Shareef Abdur-Rasheed
William S. Peters, Sr.

Our February Features
Teresa E. Gallion & Robert Gibson

the Year of the Poet
March 2014

The Poetry Posse
Jamie Bond
Gail Weston Shazor
Albert 'Infinite' Carrasco
Siddartha Beth Pierce
Janet P. Caldwell
June 'Bugg' Barefield
Debbie M. Allen
Tony Henninger
Joe DaVerbal Minddancer
Robert Gibbons
Neetu Wali
Shareef Abdur-Rasheed
Kimberly Burnham
William S. Peters, Sr.

daffodil

Our March Featured Poets
Alicia C. Cooper & hülya yılmaz

the Year of the Poet
April 2014

The Poetry Posse

Jamie Bond
Gail Weston Shazor
Albert 'Infinite' Carrasco
Siddartha Beth Pierce
Janet P. Caldwell
June 'Bugg' Barefield
Debbie M. Allen
Tony Henninger
Joe DaVerbal Minddancer
Robert Gibbons
Neetu Wali
Shareef Abdur-Rasheed
Kimberly Burnham
William S. Peters, Sr.

Our April Featured Poets
Fahredin Shehu
Martina Reisz Newberry
Justin Blackburn
Monte Smith

Sweet Pea

celebrating international poetry month

Now Available

www.innerchildpress.com/the-year-of-the-poet

the year of the poet
May 2014

May's Featured Poets

ReeCee
Joski the Poet
Shannon Stanton

Dedicated To our Children

The Poetry Posse

Jamie Bond
Gail Weston Shazor
Albert 'Infinite' Carrasco
Siddartha Beth Pierce
Janet P. Caldwell
June 'Bugg' Barefield
Debbie M. Allen
Tony Henninger
Joe DaVerbal Minddancer
Robert Gibbons
Neetu Wali
Shareef Abdur-Rasheed
Kimberly Burnham
William S. Peters, Sr.

Lily of the Valley

the Year of the Poet
June 2014

Love & Relationship

Rose

June's Featured Poets

Shanielle McLin
Jacqueline D. E. Kennedy
Abraham N. Benjamin

The Poetry Posse

Jamie Bond
Gail Weston Shazor
Albert 'Infinite' Carrasco
Siddartha Beth Pierce
Janet P. Caldwell
June 'Bugg' Barefield
Debbie M. Allen
Tony Henninger
Joe DaVerbal Minddancer
Robert Gibbons
Neetu Wali
Shareef Abdur-Rasheed
Kimberly Burnham
William S. Peters, Sr.

The Year of the Poet
July 2014

July Feature Poets

Christena A. V. Williams
Dr. John R. Strum
Kolade Olanrewaju Freedom

The Poetry Posse

Jamie Bond
Gail Weston Shazor
Siddartha Beth Pierce
Janet P. Caldwell
June 'Bugg' Barefield
Debbie M. Allen
Tony Henninger
Joe DaVerbal Minddancer
Robert Gibbons
Neetu Wali
Shareef Abdur-Rasheed
Kimberly Burnham
William S. Peters, Sr.

Lotus
Asian Flower of the Month

The Year of the Poet
August 2014

Gladiolus

The Poetry Posse

Jamie Bond
Gail Weston Shazor
Albert 'Infinite' Carrasco
Siddartha Beth Pierce
Janet P. Caldwell
June 'Bugg' Barefield
Debbie M. Allen
Tony Henninger
Joe DaVerbal Minddancer
Robert Gibbons
Neetu Wali
Shareef Abdur-Rasheed
Kimberly Burnham
William S. Peters, Sr.

August Feature Poets

Ann White * Rosalind Cherry * Sheila Jenkins

Now Available

www.innerchildpress.com/the-year-of-the-poet

The Year of the Poet
September 2014

Aster   Morning-Glory

Wild Chrysanthemum Birthday Flower

September Feature Poets
Florence Malone * Keith Alan Hamilton

The Poetry Posse
Jamie Bond * Gail Weston Shazor * Albert 'Infinite' Carrasco * Siddartha Beth Pierce
Janet P. Caldwell * June 'Bugg' Barefield * Debbie M. Allen * Tony Henninger
Joe DaVerbal Minddancer * Robert Gibbons * Neetu Wali * Shareef Abdur-Rasheed
Kimberly Burnham * William S. Peters, Sr.

THE YEAR OF THE POET
October 2014

Red Poppy

The Poetry Posse
Jamie Bond * Gail Weston Shazor * Albert 'Infinite' Carrasco * Siddartha Beth Pierce
Janet P. Caldwell * June 'Bugg' Barefield * Debbie M. Allen * Tony Henninger
Joe DaVerbal Minddancer * Robert Gibbons * Neetu Wali * Shareef Abdur-Rasheed
Kimberly Burnham * William S. Peters, Sr.

October Feature Poets
Ceri Naz * Rajendra Padhi * Elizabeth Castillo

THE YEAR OF THE POET
November 2014

Chrysanthemum

The Poetry Posse
Jamie Bond * Gail Weston Shazor * Albert 'Infinite' Carrasco * Siddartha Beth Pierce
Janet P. Caldwell * June 'Bugg' Barefield * Debbie M. Allen * Tony Henninger
Joe DaVerbal Minddancer * Robert Gibbons * Neetu Wali * Shareef Abdur-Rasheed
Kimberly Burnham * William S. Peters, Sr.

November Feature Poets
Jocelyn Mosman * Jackie Allen * James Moore * Neville Hiatt

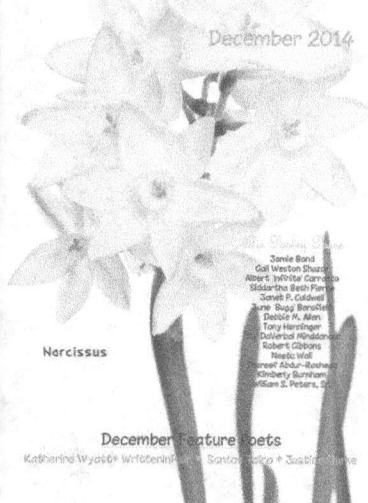

THE YEAR OF THE POET
December 2014

The Poetry Posse
Jamie Bond
Gail Weston Shazor
Albert 'Infinite' Carrasco
Siddartha Beth Pierce
Janet P. Caldwell
June 'Bugg' Barefield
Debbie M. Allen
Tony Henninger
DaVerbal Minddancer
Robert Gibbons
Neetu Wali
Shareef Abdur-Rasheed
Kimberly Burnham
William S. Peters, Sr.

Narcissus

December Feature Poets
Katherina Wyatt* Wristening* Santos Tokyo * Justin

Now Available
www.innerchildpress.com/the-year-of-the-poet

THE YEAR OF THE POET II
January 2015

Garnet

The Poetry Posse
Jamie Bond
Gail Weston Shazor
Albert 'Infinite' Carrasco
Siddartha Beth Pierce
Janet P. Caldwell
Tony Henninger
Joe DaVerbal Minddancer
Robert Gibbons
Neetu Wali
Shareef Abdur – Rasheed
Kimberly Burnham
Ann White
Keith Alan Hamilton
Katherine Wyatt
Fahredin Shehu
Hülya N. Yılmaz
Teresa E. Gallion
Jackie Allen
William S. Peters, Sr.

January Feature Poets
Bismay Mohanti * Jen Walls * Eric Judah

THE YEAR OF THE POET II
February 2015

Amethyst

THE POETRY POSSE
Jamie Bond
Gail Weston Shazor
Albert 'Infinite' Carrasco
Siddartha Beth Pierce
Janet P. Caldwell
Tony Henninger
Joe DaVerbal Minddancer
Robert Gibbons
Neetu Wali
Shareef Abdur – Rasheed
Kimberly Burnham
Ann White
Keith Alan Hamilton
Katherine Wyatt
Fahredin Shehu
Hülya N. Yılmaz
Teresa E. Gallion
Jackie Allen
William S. Peters, Sr.

FEBRUARY FEATURE POETS
Iram Fatima * Bob McNeil * Kerstin Centervall

The Year of the Poet II
March 2015

Our Featured Poets
Heung Sook * Anthony Arnold * Alicia Foland

Bloodstone

The Poetry Posse 2015
Jamie Bond * Gail Weston Shazor * Albert 'Infinite' Carrasco
Siddartha Beth Pierce * Janet P. Caldwell * Tony Henninger
Joe DaVerbal Minddancer * Neetu Wali * Shareef Abdur – Rasheed
Kimberly Burnham * Ann White * Keith Alan Hamilton
Katherine Wyatt * Fahredin Shehu * Hülya N. Yılmaz
Teresa E. Gallion * Jackie Allen * William S. Peters, Sr.

The Year of the Poet II
April 2015

Celebrating International Poetry Month

Our Featured Poets
Raja Williams * Dennis Ferado * Laure Charazac

Diamonds

The Poetry Posse 2015
Jamie Bond * Gail Weston Shazor * Albert 'Infinite' Carrasco
Siddartha Beth Pierce * Janet P. Caldwell * Tony Henninger
Joe DaVerbal Minddancer * Neetu Wali * Shareef Abdur – Rasheed
Kimberly Burnham * Ann White * Keith Alan Hamilton
Katherine Wyatt * Fahredin Shehu * Hülya N. Yılmaz
Teresa E. Gallion * Jackie Allen * William S. Peters, Sr.

Now Available

www.innerchildpress.com/the-year-of-the-poet

The Year of the Poet II
May 2015

May's Featured Poets

Geri Algeri
Akin Mosi Chinnery
Anna Jakubczak

Emeralds

The Poetry Posse 2015
Jamie Bond * Gail Weston Shazor * Albert 'Infinite' Carrasco
Siddartha Beth Pierce * Janet P. Caldwell * Tony Henninger
Joe DaVerbal Minddancer * Neetu Wali * Shareef Abdur – Rasheed
Kimberly Burnham * Ann White * Keith Alan Hamilton
Katherine Wyatt * Fahredin Shehu * Hülya N. Yılmaz
Teresa E. Gallion * Jackie Allen * William S. Peters, Sr.

The Year of the Poet II
June 2015

June's Featured Poets

Anahit Arustamyan * Yvette D. Murrell * Regina A. Walker

Pearl

The Poetry Posse 2015
Jamie Bond * Gail Weston Shazor * Albert 'Infinite' Carrasco
Siddartha Beth Pierce * Janet P. Caldwell * Tony Henninger
Joe DaVerbal Minddancer * Neetu Wali * Shareef Abdur – Rasheed
Kimberly Burnham * Ann White * Keith Alan Hamilton
Katherine Wyatt * Fahredin Shehu * Hülya N. Yılmaz
Teresa E. Gallion * Jackie Allen * William S. Peters, Sr.

The Year of the Poet II
July 2015

The Featured Poets for July 2015
Abhik Shome * Christina Neal * Robert Neal

Rubies

The Poetry Posse 2015
Jamie Bond * Gail Weston Shazor * Albert 'Infinite' Carrasco
Siddartha Beth Pierce * Janet P. Caldwell * Tony Henninger
Joe DaVerbal Minddancer * Neetu Wali * Shareef Abdur – Rasheed
Kimberly Burnham * Ann White * Keith Alan Hamilton
Katherine Wyatt * Fahredin Shehu * Hülya N. Yılmaz
Teresa E. Gallion * Jackie Allen * William S. Peters, Sr.

The Year of the Poet II
August 2015

Peridot

Featured Poets

Gayle Howell
Ann Chalasz
Christopher Schultz

The Poetry Posse 2015
Jamie Bond * Gail Weston Shazor * Albert 'Infinite' Carrasco
Siddartha Beth Pierce * Janet P. Caldwell * Tony Henninger
Joe DaVerbal Minddancer * Neetu Wali * Shareef Abdur – Rasheed
Kimberly Burnham * Ann White * Keith Alan Hamilton
Katherine Wyatt * Fahredin Shehu * Hülya N. Yılmaz
Teresa E. Gallion * Jackie Allen * William S. Peters, Sr.

Now Available

www.innerchildpress.com/the-year-of-the-poet

The Year of the Poet II
September 2015

Featured Poets
Alfreda Ghee * Lonneice Weeks Badley * Demetrios Trifiatis

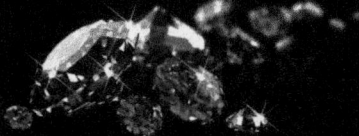

Sapphires

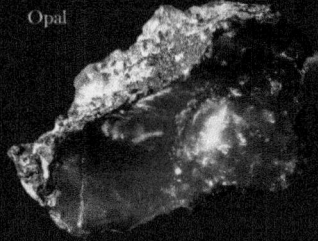

The Poetry Posse 2015
Jamie Bond * Gail Weston Shazor * Albert 'Infinite' Carrasco
Siddartha Beth Pierce * Janet P. Caldwell * Tony Henninger
Joe DaVerbal Minddancer * Neetu Wali * Shareef Abdur – Rasheed
Kimberly Burnham * Ann White * Keith Alan Hamilton
Katherine Wyatt * Fahredin Shehu * Hülya N. Yılmaz
Teresa E. Gallion * Jackie Allen * William S. Peters, Sr.

The Year of the Poet II
October 2015

Featured Poets
Monte Smith * Laura J. Wolfe * William Washington

Opal

The Poetry Posse 2015
Jamie Bond * Gail Weston Shazor * Albert 'Infinite' Carrasco
Siddartha Beth Pierce * Janet P. Caldwell * Tony Henninger
Joe DaVerbal Minddancer * Neetu Wali * Shareef Abdur – Rasheed
Kimberly Burnham * Ann White * Keith Alan Hamilton
Katherine Wyatt * Fahredin Shehu * Hülya N. Yılmaz
Teresa E. Gallion * Jackie Allen * William S. Peters, Sr.

The Year of the Poet II
November 2015

Featured Poets
Alan W. Jankowski
Bismay Mohanty
James Moore

Topaz

The Poetry Posse 2015
Jamie Bond * Gail Weston Shazor * Albert 'Infinite' Carrasco
Siddartha Beth Pierce * Janet P. Caldwell * Tony Henninger
Joe DaVerbal Minddancer * Neetu Wali * Shareef Abdur – Rasheed
Kimberly Burnham * Ann White * Keith Alan Hamilton
Katherine Wyatt * Fahredin Shehu * Hülya N. Yılmaz
Teresa E. Gallion * Jackie Allen * William S. Peters, Sr.

The Year of the Poet II
December 2015

Featured Poets
Kerione Bryan * Michelle Joan Barulich * Neville Hiatt

Turquoise

The Poetry Posse 2015
Jamie Bond * Gail Weston Shazor * Albert 'Infinite' Carrasco
Siddartha Beth Pierce * Janet P. Caldwell * Tony Henninger
Joe DaVerbal Minddancer * Neetu Wali * Shareef Abdur – Rasheed
Kimberly Burnham * Ann White * Keith Alan Hamilton
Katherine Wyatt * Fahredin Shehu * Hülya N. Yılmaz
Teresa E. Gallion * Jackie Allen * William S. Peters, Sr.

Now Available
www.innerchildpress.com/the-year-of-the-poet

The Year of the Poet III
January 2016

Featured Poets

Lana Joseph * Atom Cyrus Rush * Christena Williams

Dark-eyed Junco

The Poetry Posse 2016

The Year of the Poet III
February 2016

Featured Poets

Anthony Arnold
Anne Chalasz

Puffin

The Poetry Posse 2016

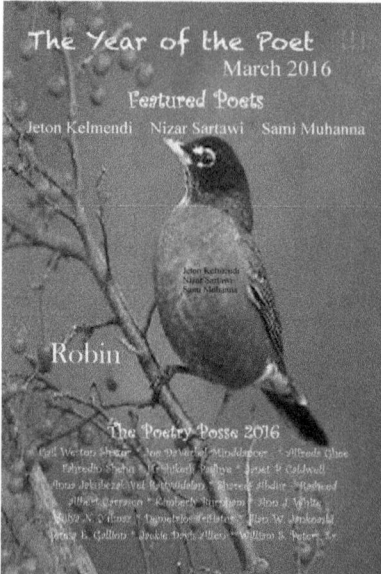

The Year of the Poet
March 2016

Featured Poets

Jeton Kelmendi   Nizar Sartawi   Sami Muhanna

Robin

The Poetry Posse 2016

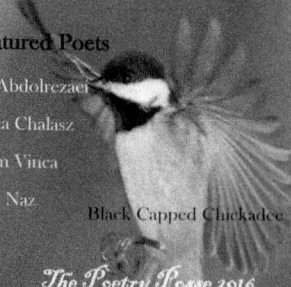

The Year of the Poet III

Featured Poets

Ali Abdolrezaei

Anna Chalasz

Agim Vinca

Ceri Naz

Black Capped Chickadee

The Poetry Posse 2016

celebrating international poetry month

Now Available

www.innerchildpress.com/the-year-of-the-poet

The Year of the Poet III
May 2016

Bob Strum
Barbara Allan
D.L. Davis

Oriole

The Year of the Poet III
June 2016

Featured Poets

Qibrije Demiri- Frangu
Naime Beqiraj
Faleeha Hassan
Bedri Zyberaj

Black Necked Stilt

The Poetry Posse 2016

The Year of the Poet III
July 2016

Featured Poets

Iram Fatima 'Ashi'
Langley Shazor
Jody Doty
Emilia T. Davis

Indigo Bunting

The Poetry Posse 2016

The Year of the Poet III
August 2016

Featured Poets

Anita Dash
Irena Jovanovic
Malgorzata Goluda

Painted Bunting

The Poetry Posse 2016

Now Available

www.innerchildpress.com/the-year-of-the-poet

205

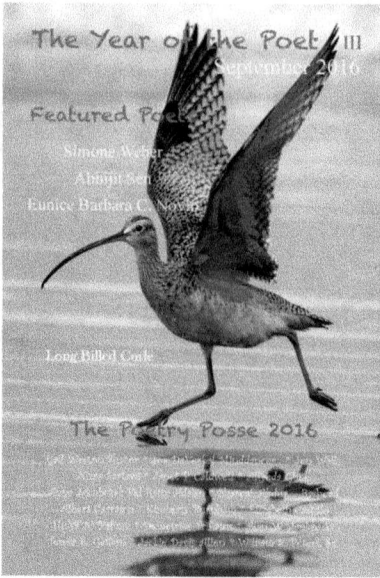

The Year of the Poet III
September 2016

Featured Poets

Simone Weber
Abhijit Sen
Eunice Barbara C. Novio

Long Billed Curle

The Poetry Posse 2016

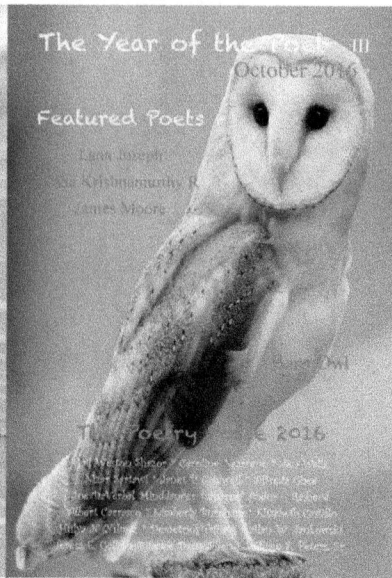

The Year of the Poet III
October 2016

Featured Poets

Laric Joseph
Asu Krishnamurthy R
James Moore

Barn Owl

The Poetry Posse 2016

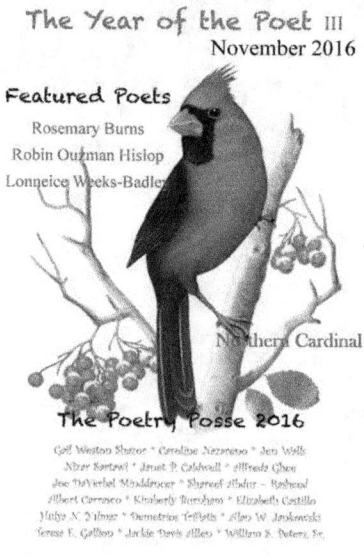

The Year of the Poet III
November 2016

Featured Poets

Rosemary Burns
Robin Ouzman Hislop
Lonneice Weeks-Badley

Northern Cardinal

The Poetry Posse 2016

Gail Weston Shazor * Caroline Nazareno * Jen Walls
Nizar Sartawi * Janet P. Caldwell * Alfreda Ghee
Joe DaVerbel Maddamma * Shareef Abdur – Rasheed
Albert Carrasco * Kimberly Burnham * Elizabeth Castillo
Hülya N. Yılmaz * Demetrios Trifiatis * Alan W. Jankowski
Teresa E. Gallion * Jackie Davis Allen * William S. Peters, Sr.

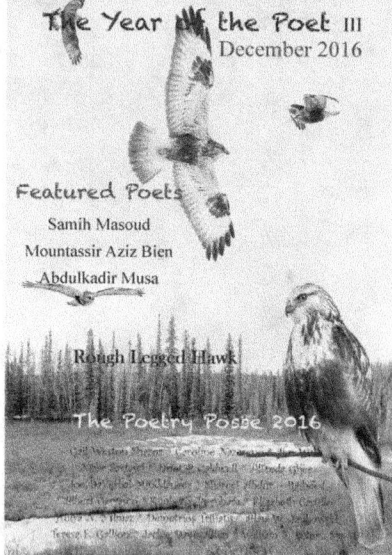

The Year of the Poet III
December 2016

Featured Poets

Samih Masoud
Mountassir Aziz Bien
Abdulkadir Musa

Rough Legged Hawk

The Poetry Posse 2016

Now Available

www.innerchildpress.com/the-year-of-the-poet

The Year of the Poet IV — January 2017

The Year of the Poet IV — February 2017

The Year of the Poet IV — March 2017

The Year of the Poet IV — April 2017

Now Available

www.innerchildpress.com/the-year-of-the-poet

The Year of the Poet IV
May 2017

The Flowering Dogwood Tree

Featured Poets
Kallisa Powell
Alicja Maria Kuberska
Fethi Sassi

The Poetry Posse 2017

Gail Weston Shazor * Caroline Nazareno * Bismay Mohanty
Teresa E. Gallion * Anna Jakubczak Vel Ratty Adalan
Joe DeVerbal Minddancer * Shareef Abdur - Rasheed
Albert Carrasco * Kimberly Burnham * Elizabeth Castillo
Hülya N. Yılmaz * Fahredin Hasani * Jackie Davis Allen
Jan Wells * Nizar Sartawi * * William S. Peters, Sr.

The Year of the Poet IV
June 2017

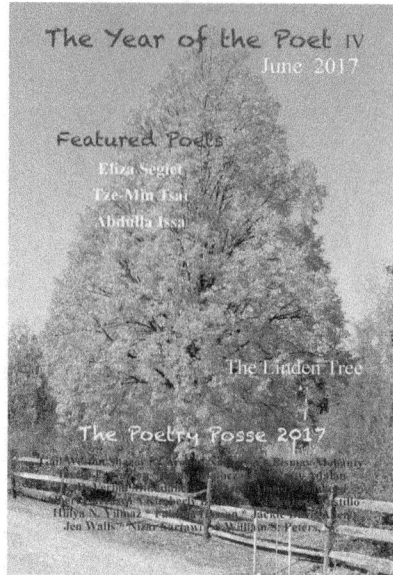

Featured Poets
Eliza Segiet
Tze-Min Tsai
Abdulla Issa

The Linden Tree

The Poetry Posse 2017

The Year of the Poet IV
July 2017

Featured Poets
Anca Mihaela Bruma
Ibaa Ismail
Zvonko Taneski

The Oak Moon

The Poetry Posse 2017

The Year of the Poet IV
August 2017

Featured Poets
Jonathan Aquino
Kitty Hsu
Langley Shazor

The Hazelnut Tree

The Poetry Posse 2017

Gail Weston Shazor * Caroline Nazareno
Teresa E. Gallion * Anna Jakubczak Vel Ratty Adalan
Joe DeVerbal Minddancer * Shareef Abdur - Rasheed
Albert Carrasco * Kimberly Burnham * Elizabeth Castillo
Hülya N. Yılmaz * Fahredin Hasani * Jackie Davis Allen
Jan Wells * Nizar Sartawi * * William S. Peters, Sr.

Now Available
www.innerchildpress.com/the-year-of-the-poet

The Year of the Poet IV
September 2017

Featured Poets

Martina Reisz Newberry
Ameer Nassir
Christine Fulco Neal
Robert Neal

The Elm Tree

The Poetry Posse 2017

Gail Weston Shazor * Caroline Nazareno * Bismay Mohanty
Teresa E. Gallion * Anna Jakubczak Vel Ratty Adalan
Joe DaVerbal Minddancer * Shareef Abdur – Rasheed
Albert Carrasco * Kimberly Burnham * Elizabeth Castillo
Hülya N. Yılmaz * Faleeha Hassan * Jackie Davis Allen
Jen Walls * Nizar Sartawi * * William S. Peters, Sr.

The Year of the Poet IV
October 2017

Featured Poets

Ahmed Abu Saleem
Nedal Al-Qaeim
Sadeddin Shahin

The Black Walnut Tree

The Poetry Posse 2017

Gail Weston Shazor * Caroline Nazareno * Bismay Mohanty
Teresa E. Gallion * Anna Jakubczak Vel Ratty Adalan
Joe DaVerbal Minddancer * Shareef Abdur – Rasheed
Albert Carrasco * Kimberly Burnham * Elizabeth Castillo
Hülya N. Yılmaz * Faleeha Hassan * Jackie Davis Allen
Jen Walls * Nizar Sartawi * * William S. Peters, Sr.

The Year of the Poet IV
November 2017

Featured Poets

Kay Peters
Alfreda D. Ghee
Gabriella Garofalo
Rosemary Cappello

The Tree of Life

The Poetry Posse 2017

Gail Weston Shazor * Caroline Nazareno * Bismay Mohanty
Teresa E. Gallion * Anna Jakubczak Vel Ratty Adalan
Joe DaVerbal Minddancer * Shareef Abdur – Rasheed
Albert Carrasco * Kimberly Burnham * Elizabeth Castillo
Hülya N. Yılmaz * Faleeha Hassan * Jackie Davis Allen
Jen Walls * Nizar Sartawi * William S. Peters, Sr.

The Year of the Poet IV
December 2017

Featured Poets

Justice Clarke
Mariel M. Pabroa
Kiley Brown

The Fig Tree

The Poetry Posse 2017

Gail Weston Shazor * Caroline Nazareno * Bismay Mohanty
Teresa E. Gallion * Anna Jakubczak Vel Ratty Adalan
Joe DaVerbal Minddancer * Shareef Abdur – Rasheed
Albert Carrasco * Kimberly Burnham * Elizabeth Castillo
Hülya N. Yılmaz * Faleeha Hassan * Jackie Davis Allen
Jen Walls * Nizar Sartawi * William S. Peters, Sr.

Now Available

www.innerchildpress.com/the-year-of-the-poet

The Year of the Poet V

January 2018

Featured Poets

Iyad Shamasnah

Yasmeen Hamzeh

Ali Abdolrezaei

Aksum

The Poetry Posse 2018

Gail Weston Shazor * Caroline Nazareno * Tezmin Ition Tsai
Hülya N. Yılmaz * Faleeha Hassan * Jackie Davis Allen
Teresa E. Gallion * Anna Jakubczak Vel Ratty Adalan
Alicja Maria Kuberska * Shareef Abdur – Rasheed
Kimberly Burnham * Elizabeth Castillo
Nizar Sartawi * William S. Peters, Sr.

The Year of the Poet V

February 2018

Sabean

Featured Poets

Muhammad Azram

Anna Szawracka

Abhilipsa Kumar

Aanika Aery

The Poetry Posse 2018

Gail Weston Shazor * Caroline Nazareno * Tezmin Ition Tsai
Hülya N. Yılmaz * Faleeha Hassan * Jackie Davis Allen
Teresa E. Gallion * Anna Jakubczak Vel Ratty Adalan
Alicja Maria Kuberska * Shareef Abdur – Rasheed
Kimberly Burnham * Elizabeth Castillo
Nizar Sartawi * William S. Peters, Sr.

The Year of the Poet V

March 2018

Featured Poets

Iram Fatima 'Ashi'
Cassandra Swan
Jaleel Khazaal
Shazia Zaman

Caribbean
&
Middle America

The Poetry Posse 2018

Gail Weston Shazor * Nizar Sartawi * Hülya N. Yılmaz
Jackie Davis Allen * Caroline 'Ceri' Nazareno
Alicja Maria Kuberska * Teresa E. Gallion
Faleeha Hassan * Shareef Abdur – Rasheed
Kimberly Burnham * Elizabeth Castillo
Tezmin Ition Tsai * William S. Peters, Sr.

The Year of the Poet V

April 2018

Featured Poets

The Nez Perce

The Poetry Posse 2018

Now Available

www.innerchildpress.com/the-year-of-the-poet

The Year of the Poet V
May 2018

Featured Poets
Zaldy Carreon de Leon Jr.
Sylwia K. Malinowska
Landita Ahmeti
Otelia Prodan
The Sumerians

The Poetry Posse 2018
Gail Weston Shazor * Nizar Sartawi * Hülya N. Yılmaz
Jackie Davis Allen * Caroline 'Ceri' Nazareno
Alicja Maria Kuberska * Teresa E. Gallion
Kimberly Burnham * Shareef Abdur – Rasheed
Faleeha Hassan * Elizabeth Castillo * Swapna Behera
Tezmin Ition Tsai * William S. Peters, Sr.

The Year of the Poet V
June 2018

Featured Poets
Bilall Maliqi * Daim Miftari * Gojko Božović * Sofija Živković

The Paleo Indians

The Poetry Posse 2018
Gail Weston Shazor * Nizar Sartawi * Hülya N. Yılmaz
Jackie Davis Allen * Caroline 'Ceri' Nazareno
Alicja Maria Kuberska * Teresa E. Gallion
Kimberly Burnham * Shareef Abdur – Rasheed
Faleeha Hassan * Elizabeth Castillo * Swapna Behera
Tezmin Ition Tsai * William S. Peters, Sr.

The Year of the Poet V
July 2018

Featured Poets
Patinaja Irenger-Paddy
Mohammad Ekbal Hazm
Eliza Segiet
Tom Higgins

Oceania

The Poetry Posse 2018
Gail Weston Shazor * Nizar Sartawi * Hülya N. Yılmaz
Jackie Davis Allen * Caroline 'Ceri' Nazareno
Alicja Maria Kuberska * Teresa E. Gallion
Kimberly Burnham * Shareef Abdur – Rasheed
Faleeha Hassan * Elizabeth Castillo * Swapna Behera
Tezmin Ition Tsai * William S. Peters, Sr.

The Year of the Poet V
August 2018

Featured Poets
Hussein Habasch * Mircea Dan Duta * Naida Mujkić * Swagat Das

The Lapita

The Poetry Posse 2018
Gail Weston Shazor * Nizar Sartawi * Hülya N. Yılmaz
Jackie Davis Allen * Caroline 'Ceri' Nazareno
Alicja Maria Kuberska * Teresa E. Gallion
Kimberly Burnham * Shareef Abdur – Rasheed
Ashok K. Bhargava* Elizabeth Castillo * Swapna Behaera
Tezmin Ition Tsai * William S. Peters, Sr.

Now Available

www.innerchildpress.com/the-year-of-the-poet

The Year of the Poet V
September 2018

The Aztecs & Incas

Featured Poets

Joshide Olanrewaju Freedom
Eliza Segiet
Mother Hannton Abdul Ghoni
Lilly Swaim

The Poetry Posse 2018

Gail Weston Shazor * Nizar Sartawi * Hülya N. Yılmaz
Jackie Davis Allen * Caroline 'Ceri' Nazareno
Alicja Maria Kubenska * Teresa E. Gallion
Kimberly Burnham * Shareef Abdur – Rasheed
Ashok K. Bhargava * Elizabeth Castillo * Swapna Behera
Tezmin Ition Tsai * William S. Peters, Sr.

The Year of the Poet V
October 2018

Featured Poets
Alicia Minjarez * Lenneike Weeks-Badley
Lopamudra Mishra * Abdelwahed Souayah

Bengali

The Poetry Posse 2018

Gail Weston Shazor * Nizar Sartawi * Hülya N. Yılmaz
Jackie Davis Allen * Caroline 'Ceri' Nazareno
Alicja Maria Kubenska * Teresa E. Gallion
Kimberly Burnham * Shareef Abdur – Rasheed
Ashok K. Bhargava * Elizabeth Castillo * Swapna Behera
Tezmin Ition Tsai * William S. Peters, Sr.

The Year of the Poet V
November 2018

Featured Poets
Michelle Joan Barulich * Monsif Beroual
Krystyna Konecka * Nassira Nezzar

The Poetry Posse 2018

Gail Weston Shazor * Nizar Sartawi * Hülya N. Yılmaz
Jackie Davis Allen * Caroline 'Ceri' Nazareno
Alicja Maria Kubenska * Teresa E. Gallion
Kimberly Burnham * Shareef Abdur – Rasheed
Ashok K. Bhargava * Elizabeth Castillo * Swapna Behera
Tezmin Ition Tsai * William S. Peters, Sr.

The Year of the Poet V
December 2018

Featured Poets
Rose Terranova Cirigliano
Joanna Kalinowska
Sokolović Emin
Dr. T. Ashok Chakravarthy

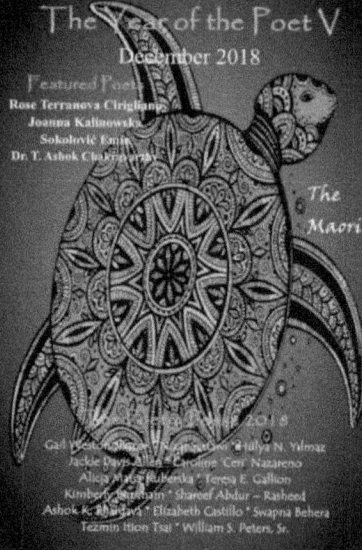

The Maori

The Poetry Posse 2018

Gail Weston Shazor * Nizar Sartawi * Hülya N. Yılmaz
Jackie Davis Allen * Caroline 'Ceri' Nazareno
Alicja Maria Kubenska * Teresa E. Gallion
Kimberly Burnham * Shareef Abdur – Rasheed
Ashok K. Bhargava * Elizabeth Castillo * Swapna Behera
Tezmin Ition Tsai * William S. Peters, Sr.

Now Available
www.innerchildpress.com/the-year-of-the-poet

The Year of the Poet VI
January 2019

Indigenous North Americans

Featured Poets

Houda Elfchtali
Anthony Brisene
Iram Fatima 'Ashi'
Dr. K. K. Mathew

Dream Catcher

The Poetry Posse 2019

Gail Weston Shazor * Joe Paire * Hülya N. Yılmaz
Jackie Davis Allen * Caroline 'Ceri' Nazareno
Alicja Maria Kubenska * Teresa E. Gallion
Kimberly Burnham * Shareef Abdur – Rasheed
Ashok K. Bhargava * Elizabeth Castillo * Swapna Behera
Tezmin Ition Tsai * William S. Peters, Sr.

The Year of the Poet VI
February 2019

Featured Poets

Marek Lukaszewicz * Bharati Nayak
Aida G. Roque * Jean-Jacques Fournier

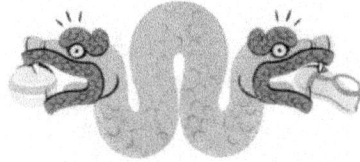

Meso-America

The Poetry Posse 2019

Gail Weston Shazor * Albert Carrasco * Hülya N. Yılmaz
Jackie Davis Allen * Caroline Nazareno * Eliza Segiet
Alicja Maria Kubenska * Teresa E. Gallion * Joe Paire
Kimberly Burnham * shareef Abdur – Rasheed
Ashok K. Bhargava * Elizabeth Castillo * Swapna Behera
Tezmin Ition Tsai * William S. Peters, Sr.

The Year of the Poet VI
March 2019

Featured Poets

Enesa Mahmić * Sylwia K. Malinovska
Shuruik Hammoud * Anwer Ghani

The Caribbean

The Poetry Posse 2019

Gail Weston Shazor * Albert Carrasco * Hülya N. Yılmaz
Jackie Davis Allen * Caroline Nazareno * Eliza Segiet
Alicja Maria Kubenska * Teresa E. Gallion * Joe Paire
Kimberly Burnham * Shareef Abdur – Rasheed
Ashok K. Bhargava * Elizabeth Castillo * Swapna Behera
Tezmin Ition Tsai * William S. Peters, Sr.

The Year of the Poet VI
April 2019

Featured Poets

DL Davis * Michelle Joan Barulich
Lulëzim Haziri * Faleeha Hassan

Central & West Africa

The Poetry Posse 2019

Gail Weston Shazor * Albert Carrasco * Hülya N. Yılmaz
Jackie Davis Allen * Caroline Nazareno * Eliza Segiet
Alicja Maria Kubenska * Teresa E. Gallion * Joe Paire
Kimberly Burnham * Shareef Abdur – Rasheed
Ashok K. Bhargava * Elizabeth Castillo * Swapna Behera
Tezmin Ition Tsai * William S. Peters, Sr.

Now Available

www.innerchildpress.com/the-year-of-the-poet

The Year of the Poet VI
May 2019

Featured Poets

Emad Al-Haydary * Hussein Nasser Jabr
Wahab Sheriff * Abdul Razzaq Al Ameeri

Asia Southeast Asia and Maritime Asia

The Poetry Posse 2019

Gail Weston Shazor * Albert Carrasco * Hülya N. Yılmaz
Jackie Davis Allen * Caroline Nazareno * Eliza Segiet
Alicja Maria Kuberska * Teresa E. Gallion * Joe Paire
Kimberly Burnham * Shareef Abdur – Rasheed
Ashok K. Bhargava * Elizabeth Castillo * Swapna Behera
Tezmin Ition Tsai * William S. Peters, Sr.

The Year of the Poet VI
June 2019

Featured Poets

Kate Gaudi Powiekszone * Sahaj Sabharwal
Iwu Jeff * Mohamed Abdel Aziz Shneis

Arctic Circumpolar

The Poetry Posse 2019

Gail Weston Shazor * Albert Carrasco * Hülya N. Yılmaz
Jackie Davis Allen * Caroline Nazareno * Eliza Segiet
Alicja Maria Kuberska * Teresa E. Gallion * Joe Paire
Kimberly Burnham * Shareef Abdur – Rasheed
Ashok K. Bhargava * Elizabeth Castillo * Swapna Behera
Tezmin Ition Tsai * William S. Peters, Sr.

The Year of the Poet VI
July 2019

Featured Poets

Saadeddin Shahin * Andy Scott
Fahredin Shehu * Alok Kumar Ray

The Horn of Africa

Ethiopia   Djibouti

Somalia   EriTrea

The Poetry Posse 2019

Gail Weston Shazor * Albert Carrasco * Hülya N. Yılmaz
Jackie Davis Allen * Caroline Nazareno * Eliza Segiet
Alicja Maria Kuberska * Teresa E. Gallion * Joe Paire
Kimberly Burnham * Shareef Abdur – Rasheed
Ashok K. Bhargava * Elizabeth Castillo * Swapna Behera
Tezmin Ition Tsai * William S. Peters, Sr.

The Year of the Poet VI
August 2019

Featured Poets

Shola Balogun * Bharati Nayak
Monalisa Dash Dwibedy * Mbizo Chirasha

CoExist

Southwest Asia

The Poetry Posse 2019

Gail Weston Shazor * Albert Carrasco * Hülya N. Yılmaz
Jackie Davis Allen * Caroline Nazareno * Eliza Segiet
Alicja Maria Kuberska * Teresa E. Gallion * Joe Paire
Kimberly Burnham * Shareef Abdur – Rasheed
Ashok K. Bhargava * Elizabeth Castillo * Swapna Behera
Tezmin Ition Tsai * William S. Peters, Sr.

Now Available

www.innerchildpress.com/the-year-of-the-poet

The Year of the Poet VI
September 2019
Featured Poets
Elena Liliana Popescu * Gobinda Biswas
Iram Fatima 'Ashi' * Joseph S. Spence, Sr
The Caucasus
The Poetry Posse 2019

The Year of the Poet VI
October 2019
Featured Poets
Ngozi Olivia Osuoha * Denisa Kondic
Parikhun Sinha * Christena AV Williams
The Nile Valley
The Poetry Posse 2019

The Year of the Poet VI
November 2019
Featured Poets
Rozalia Aleksandrova * Ominulu Giongo
Seimili Ranjan Mohanty * Sofia Skleida
Northern Asia
The Poetry Posse 2019

The Year of the Poet VI
December 2019
Featured Poets
Bankim Warrick Karmavir * Smriti Patil
Bharati Nayak * Kapardeli Eftichia
Oceania
The Poetry Posse 2019

Now Available

www.innerchildpress.com/the-year-of-the-poet

The Year of the Poet VII
January 2020
Featured Poets
B S Tyagi * Ashok Chakravarthy Tholana
Andy Scott * Anwer Ghani

1901 Jean Henry Dunant and Frédéric Passy

The Year of Peace
Celebrating past Nobel Peace Prize Recipients

The Poetry Posse 2020
Gail Weston Shazor * Albert Carasco * Hülya N. Yılmaz
Jackie Davis Allen * Caroline Nazareno * Eliza Segiet
Alicja Maria Kuberska * Teresa E. Gallion * Joe Paire
Kimberly Burnham * Shareef Abdur – Rasheed
Ashok K. Bhargava * Elizabeth Castillo * Swapna Behera
Tezmin Ition Tsai * William S. Peters, Sr.

The Year of the Poet VII
February 2020
Featured Poets
Jennifer Ades * Martina Reisz Newberry
Ibrahim Honjo * Claudia Piccinno

Henri La Fontaine ~ 1913

The Year of Peace
Celebrating past Nobel Peace Prize Recipients

The Poetry Posse 2020
Gail Weston Shazor * Albert Carasco * Hülya N. Yılmaz
Jackie Davis Allen * Caroline Nazareno * Eliza Segiet
Alicja Maria Kuberska * Teresa E. Gallion * Joe Paire
Kimberly Burnham * Shareef Abdur – Rasheed
Ashok K. Bhargava * Elizabeth Castillo * Swapna Behera
Tezmin Ition Tsai * William S. Peters, Sr.

The Year of the Poet VII
March 2020
Featured Poets
Aziz Mountassir * Krishna Paraisa
Hannie Rouweler * Rozalia Aleksandrova

Aristide Briand ~ 1926 ~ Gustav Stresemann

The Year of Peace
Celebrating past Nobel Peace Prize Recipients

The Poetry Posse 2020
Gail Weston Shazor * Albert Carasco * Hülya N. Yılmaz
Jackie Davis Allen * Caroline Nazareno * Eliza Segiet
Alicja Maria Kuberska * Teresa E. Gallion * Joe Paire
Kimberly Burnham * Shareef Abdur – Rasheed
Ashok K. Bhargava * Elizabeth Castillo * Swapna Behera
Tezmin Ition Tsai * William S. Peters, Sr.

The Year of the Poet VII
April 2020
Featured Poets
Rohini Behera * Mircea Dan Duta
Monalisa Dash Dwibedy * NilavroNill Shoovro

Carlos Saavedra Lamas ~ 1936

The Year of Peace
Celebrating past Nobel Peace Prize Recipients

The Poetry Posse 2020
Gail Weston Shazor * Albert Carasco * Hülya N. Yılmaz
Jackie Davis Allen * Caroline Nazareno * Eliza Segiet
Alicja Maria Kuberska * Teresa E. Gallion * Joe Paire
Kimberly Burnham * Shareef Abdur – Rasheed
Ashok K. Bhargava * Elizabeth Castillo * Swapna Behera
Tezmin Ition Tsai * William S. Peters, Sr.

Now Available
www.innerchildpress.com/the-year-of-the-poet

The Year of the Poet VII
May 2020

Featured Poets
Alok Kumar Ray * Eden S. Trinidad
Franco Barbato * Izabela Zubko

Ralph Bunche ~ 1950

The Year of Peace
Celebrating past Nobel Peace Prize Recipients

The Poetry Posse 2020

Gail Weston Shazor * Albert Carasco * Hülya N. Yılmaz
Jackie Davis Allen * Caroline Nazareno * Eliza Segiet
Alicja Maria Kuberska * Teresa E. Gallion * Joe Paire
Kimberly Burnham * Shareef Abdur – Rasheed
Ashok K. Bhargava * Elizabeth Castillo * Swapna Behera
Tezmin Ition Tsai * William S. Peters, Sr.

The Year of the Poet VII
June 2020

Featured Poets
Eftichia Kapardeli * Metin Cengiz
Hussein Habasch * Kosh K Mathew

Albert John Lutuli ~ 1960

The Year of Peace
Celebrating past Nobel Peace Prize Recipients

The Poetry Posse 2020

Gail Weston Shazor * Albert Carasco * Hülya N. Yılmaz
Jackie Davis Allen * Caroline Nazareno * Eliza Segiet
Alicja Maria Kuberska * Teresa E. Gallion * Joe Paire
Kimberly Burnham * Shareef Abdur – Rasheed
Ashok K. Bhargava * Elizabeth Castillo * Swapna Behera
Tezmin Ition Tsai * William S. Peters, Sr.

The Year of the Poet VII
July 2020

Featured Poets
Mykola Martyniuk * Orbindu Ganga
Roula Pollard * Karn Praktisha

Norman Ernest Borlaug ~ 1970

The Year of Peace
Celebrating past Nobel Peace Prize Recipients

The Poetry Posse 2020

Gail Weston Shazor * Albert Carasco * Hülya N. Yılmaz
Jackie Davis Allen * Caroline Nazareno * Eliza Segiet
Alicja Maria Kuberska * Teresa E. Gallion * Joe Paire
Kimberly Burnham * Shareef Abdur – Rasheed
Ashok K. Bhargava * Elizabeth Castillo * Swapna Behera
Tezmin Ition Tsai * William S. Peters, Sr.

The Year of the Poet VII
August 2020

Featured Poets
Dr Pragya Suman * Chinh Nguyen
Srinivas Vasudev * Ugwu Leonard Ifeanyi, Jr.

Adolfo Pérez Esquivel ~ 1980

The Year of Peace
Celebrating past Nobel Peace Prize Recipients

The Poetry Posse 2020

Gail Weston Shazor * Albert Carasco * Hülya N. Yılmaz
Jackie Davis Allen * Caroline Nazareno * Eliza Segiet
Alicja Maria Kuberska * Teresa E. Gallion * Joe Paire
Kimberly Burnham * Shareef Abdur – Rasheed
Ashok K. Bhargava * Elizabeth Castillo * Swapna Behera
Tezmin Ition Tsai * William S. Peters, Sr.

Now Available

www.innerchildpress.com/the-year-of-the-poet

The Year of the Poet VII

September 2020

Featured Poets

Raed Anis Al-Jishi * Selkinovic Smrzimi
Dr. Renesh Kumar Gupta * Umid Najjari

Mikhail Sergeyevich Gorbachev ~ 1990

The Year of Peace
Celebrating past Nobel Peace Prize Recipients

The Poetry Posse 2020

Gail Weston Shazor * Albert Carasco * Hülya N. Yilmaz
Jackie Davis Allen * Caroline Nazareno * Eliza Segiet
Alicja Maria Kuberska * Teresa E. Gallion * Joe Paire
Kimberly Burnham * Shareef Abdur – Rasheed
Ashok K. Bhargava * Elizabeth Castillo * Swapna Behera
Tezmin Ition Tsai * William S. Peters, Sr.

The Year of the Poet VII

October 2020

Featured Poets

Mutawaf A. Shaheed * Galina Italyanskaya
Nadeem Fraz * Avril Tanya Meallem

Kim Dae-jung ~ 2000

The Year of Peace
Celebrating past Nobel Peace Prize Recipients

The Poetry Posse 2020

Gail Weston Shazor * Albert Carasco * Hülya N. Yilmaz
Jackie Davis Allen * Caroline Nazareno * Eliza Segiet
Alicja Maria Kuberska * Teresa E. Gallion * Joe Paire
Kimberly Burnham * Shareef Abdur – Rasheed
Ashok K. Bhargava * Elizabeth Castillo * Swapna Behera
Tezmin Ition Tsai * William S. Peters, Sr.

The Year of the Poet VII

November 2020

Featured Poets

Elisa Mascia * Sue Lindenberg McClelland
Hatif Janabi * Ivan Gaćina

Liu Xiaobo ~ 2010

The Year of Peace
Celebrating past Nobel Peace Prize Recipients

The Poetry Posse 2020

Gail Weston Shazor * Albert Carasco * Hülya N. Yilmaz
Jackie Davis Allen * Caroline Nazareno * Eliza Segiet
Alicja Maria Kuberska * Teresa E. Gallion * Joe Paire
Kimberly Burnham * Shareef Abdur – Rasheed
Ashok K. Bhargava * Elizabeth Castillo * Swapna Behera
Tezmin Ition Tsai * William S. Peters, Sr.

The Year of the Poet VII

December 2020

Featured Poets

Ratan Ghosh * Ibtisam Ibrahim Al-Asady
Brindha Vinodh * Selma Kopic

Abiy Ahmed Ali ~ 2019

The Year of Peace
Celebrating past Nobel Peace Prize Recipients

The Poetry Posse 2020

Gail Weston Shazor * Albert Carasco * Hülya N. Yilmaz
Jackie Davis Allen * Caroline Nazareno * Eliza Segiet
Alicja Maria Kuberska * Teresa E. Gallion * Joe Paire
Kimberly Burnham * Shareef Abdur – Rasheed
Ashok K. Bhargava * Elizabeth Castillo * Swapna Behera
Tezmin Ition Tsai * William S. Peters, Sr.

Now Available

www.innerchildpress.com/the-year-of-the-poet

The Year of the Poet VIII

January 2021

Featured Global Poets
Andrew Scott * Debaprasanna Biswas
Shakil Kalam * Changming Yuan

Banksy's The Girl with the Pierced Eardrum

Poetry ... Ekphrasticly Speaking

The Poetry Posse 2020
Gail Weston Shazor * Albert Carasso * Hülya N. Yılmaz
Jackie Davis Allen * Caroline Nazareno * Eliza Segiet
Alicja Maria Kuberska * Teresa E. Gallion * Joe Paire
Kimberly Burnham * Shareef Abdur – Rasheed
Ashok K. Bhargava * Elizabeth Castillo * Swapna Behera
Tezmin Ition Tsai * William S. Peters, Sr.

The Year of the Poet VIII

February 2021

Featured Global Poets
T. Ramesh Babu * Ruchida Barman
Neptune Barman * Faleeha Hassan

Emory Douglas : 1968 Olympics mural

Poetry ... Ekphrasticly Speaking

The Poetry Posse 2021
Gail Weston Shazor * Albert Carasso * Hülya N. Yılmaz
Jackie Davis Allen * Caroline Nazareno * Eliza Segiet
Alicja Maria Kuberska * Teresa E. Gallion * Joe Paire
Kimberly Burnham * Shareef Abdur – Rasheed
Ashok K. Bhargava * Elizabeth Castillo * Swapna Behera
Tezmin Ition Tsai * William S. Peters, Sr.

The Year of the Poet VIII

March 2021

Featured Global Poets
Claudia Piccinno * Mohammed Jabr
Luzviminda Rivera * Nigar Arif

Tatyana Fazlalizadeh

Poetry ... Ekphrasticly Speaking

The Poetry Posse 2021
Gail Weston Shazor * Albert Carasso * Hülya N. Yılmaz
Jackie Davis Allen * Caroline Nazareno * Eliza Segiet
Alicja Maria Kuberska * Teresa E. Gallion * Joe Paire
Kimberly Burnham * Shareef Abdur – Rasheed
Ashok K. Bhargava * Elizabeth Castillo * Swapna Behera
Tezmin Ition Tsai * William S. Peters, Sr.

The Year of the Poet VIII

April 2021

Featured Global Poets
Katarzyna Brus- Sawczuk * Anwesha Paul
Rozalia Aleksandrova * Shahid Abbas

Pablo O'Higgins

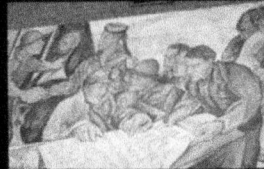

Poetry ... Ekphrasticly Speaking

The Poetry Posse 2021
Gail Weston Shazor * Albert Carasso * Hülya N. Yılmaz
Jackie Davis Allen * Caroline Nazareno * Eliza Segiet
Alicja Maria Kuberska * Teresa E. Gallion * Joe Paire
Kimberly Burnham * Shareef Abdur – Rasheed
Ashok K. Bhargava * Elizabeth Castillo * Swapna Behera
Tezmin Ition Tsai * William S. Peters, Sr.

Now Available

www.innerchildpress.com/the-year-of-the-poet

The Year of the Poet VIII

May 2021

Featured Global Poets

Paramita Mukherjee Mullick * Rose Zerguine
Jaydeep Sarangi * Bismay Mohanty

Diego Rivera

Poetry ... Ekphrasticly Speaking

The Poetry Posse 2021

Gail Weston Shazor * Albert Carassco * Hülya N. Yılmaz
Jackie Davis Allen * Caroline Nazareno * Eliza Segiet
Alicja Maria Kuberska * Teresa E. Gallion * Joe Paire
Kimberly Burnham * Shareef Abdur – Rasheed
Ashok K. Bhargava * Elizabeth Castillo * Swapna Behera
Tezmin Ition Tsai * William S. Peters, Sr.

The Year of the Poet VIII

June 2021

Featured Global Poets

Alonzo "zO" Gross * Lali Tsipi Michaeli
Tareq al Karmy * Tirthendu Ganguly

Rayen Kang

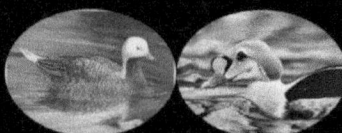

Poetry ... Ekphrasticly Speaking

The Poetry Posse 2021

Gail Weston Shazor * Albert Carassco * Hülya N. Yılmaz
Jackie Davis Allen * Caroline Nazareno * Eliza Segiet
Alicja Maria Kuberska * Teresa E. Gallion * Joe Paire
Kimberly Burnham * Shareef Abdur – Rasheed
Ashok K. Bhargava * Elizabeth Castillo * Swapna Behera
Tezmin Ition Tsai * William S. Peters, Sr.

The Year of the Poet VIII

July 2021

Featured Global Poets

Iram Jaan * Vesna Mundishevska-Veljanovska
Ngozi Olivia Osuoha * Lan Qyqalla

Goncalao Mabunda

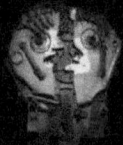

Poetry ... Ekphrasticly Speaking

The Poetry Posse 2021

Gail Weston Shazor * Albert Carassco * Hülya N. Yılmaz
Jackie Davis Allen * Caroline Nazareno * Eliza Segiet
Alicja Maria Kuberska * Teresa E. Gallion * Joe Paire
Kimberly Burnham * Shareef Abdur – Rasheed
Ashok K. Bhargava * Elizabeth Castillo * Swapna Behera
Tezmin Ition Tsai * William S. Peters, Sr.

The Year of the Poet VIII

August 2021

Featured Global Poets

Caroline Laurent Turunc * Kamal Dhungana
Pankhuri Sinha * Paramita Mukherjee Mullick

Mundara Koorang

Poetry ... Ekphrasticly Speaking

The Poetry Posse 2021

Gail Weston Shazor * Albert Carassco * Hülya N. Yılmaz
Jackie Davis Allen * Caroline Nazareno * Eliza Segiet
Alicja Maria Kuberska * Teresa E. Gallion * Joe Paire
Kimberly Burnham * Shareef Abdur – Rasheed
Ashok K. Bhargava * Elizabeth Castillo * Swapna Behera
Tezmin Ition Tsai * William S. Peters, Sr.

Now Available

www.innerchildpress.com/the-year-of-the-poet

The Year of the Poet VIII
September 2021
Featured Global Poets
Monsif Beroual * Sandesh Ghimire

Sharmila Poudel * Pavol Janik

Heather Jansch

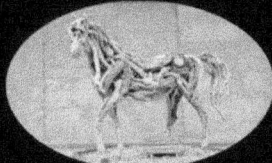

Poetry ... Ekphrasticly Speaking

The Poetry Posse 2021
Gail Weston Shazor * Albert Carasco * Hülya N. Yilmaz
Jackie Davis Allen * Caroline Nazareno * Eliza Segiet
Alicja Maria Kuberska * Teresa E. Gallion * Joe Paire
Kimberly Burnham * Shareef Abdur – Rasheed
Ashok K. Bhargava * Elizabeth Castillo * Swapna Behera
Tezmin Ition Tsai * William S. Peters, Sr.

The Year of the Poet VIII
October 2021
Featured Global Poets
C. E. Shy * Saswata Ganguly
Suranjit Gain * Hasiba Hilal

Dale Lamphere

Poetry ... Ekphrasticly Speaking

The Poetry Posse 2021
Gail Weston Shazor * Albert Carasco * Hülya N. Yilmaz
Jackie Davis Allen * Caroline Nazareno * Eliza Segiet
Alicja Maria Kuberska * Teresa E. Gallion * Joe Paire
Kimberly Burnham * Shareef Abdur – Rasheed
Ashok K. Bhargava * Elizabeth Castillo * Swapna Behera
Tezmin Ition Tsai * William S. Peters, Sr.

The Year of the Poet VIII
November 2021
Featured Global Poets
Errol D. Bean * Ibrahim Honjo
Tanja Ajtic * Rajashree Mohapatra

Andy Goldsworthy

Poetry ... Ekphrasticly Speaking

The Poetry Posse 2021
Gail Weston Shazor * Albert Carasco * Hülya N. Yilmaz
Jackie Davis Allen * Caroline Nazareno * Eliza Segiet
Alicja Maria Kuberska * Teresa E. Gallion * Joe Paire
Kimberly Burnham * Shareef Abdur – Rasheed
Ashok K. Bhargava * Elizabeth Castillo * Swapna Behera
Tezmin Ition Tsai * William S. Peters, Sr.

The Year of the Poet VIII
December 2021
Featured Global Poets
Orbinda Ganga * Fadairo Tesleem
Anthony Arnold * Iyad Shamasnah

Fredric Edwin Church

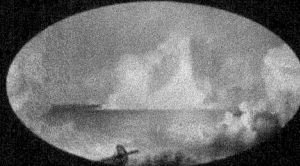

Poetry ... Ekphrasticly Speaking

The Poetry Posse 2021
Gail Weston Shazor * Albert Carasco * Hülya N. Yilmaz
Jackie Davis Allen * Caroline Nazareno * Eliza Segiet
Alicja Maria Kuberska * Teresa E. Gallion * Joe Paire
Kimberly Burnham * Shareef Abdur – Rasheed
Ashok K. Bhargava * Elizabeth Castillo * Swapna Behera
Tezmin Ition Tsai * William S. Peters, Sr.

Now Available

www.innerchildpress.com/the-year-of-the-poet

The Year of the Poet IX
January 2022

Featured Global Poets
**Ratan Ghosh * Christine Neil-Wright
Andrew Scott * Ashok Kumar**

Climate Change : The Ice Cap

Poetry . . . Ekphrasticly Speaking

The Poetry Posse 2021

Gail Weston Shazor * Albert Carasco * Hülya N. Yılmaz
Jackie Davis Allen * Caroline Nazareno * Eliza Segiet
Alicja Maria Kuberska * Teresa E. Gallion * Joe Paire
Kimberly Burnham * Shareef Abdur – Rasheed
Ashok K. Bhargava * Elizabeth Castillo * Swapna Behera
Tezmin Ition Tsai * William S. Peters, Sr.

The Year of the Poet IX
February 2022

Featured Global Poets
Roza Boyanova * Ramón de Jesús Núñez Duval
Mammad Ismayil * Tarana Turan Rahimli

Climate Change and Mountains

Poetry . . . Ekphrasticly Speaking

The Poetry Posse 2021

Gail Weston Shazor * Albert Carasco * Hülya N. Yılmaz
Jackie Davis Allen * Caroline Nazareno * Eliza Segiet
Alicja Maria Kuberska * Teresa E. Gallion * Joe Paire
Kimberly Burnham * Shareef Abdur – Rasheed
Ashok K. Bhargava * Elizabeth Castillo * Swapna Behera
Tezmin Ition Tsai * William S. Peters, Sr.

The Year of the Poet IX
March 2022

Featured Global Poets
Dimitris P. Kraniotis * Marlene Pasini
Kennedy Ochieng * Swayam Prashant

Climate Change and Space Debris

Poetry . . . Ekphrasticly Speaking

The Poetry Posse 2021

Gail Weston Shazor * Albert Carasco * Hülya N. Yılmaz
Jackie Davis Allen * Caroline Nazareno * Eliza Segiet
Alicja Maria Kuberska * Teresa E. Gallion * Joe Paire
Kimberly Burnham * Shareef Abdur – Rasheed
Ashok K. Bhargava * Elizabeth Castillo * Swapna Behera
Tezmin Ition Tsai * William S. Peters, Sr.

The Year of the Poet IX
April 2022

Featured Global Poets
**Alonzo Gross * Dr. Debaprasanna Biswas
Monsif Beroual * Carol Aronoff**

Climate Change and Oceans

*Celebrating our 100th Edition *

Poetry . . . Ekphrasticly Speaking

The Poetry Posse 2021

Gail Weston Shazor * Albert Carasco * Hülya N. Yılmaz
Jackie Davis Allen * Caroline Nazareno * Eliza Segiet
Alicja Maria Kuberska * Teresa E. Gallion * Joe Paire
Kimberly Burnham * Shareef Abdur – Rasheed
Ashok K. Bhargava * Elizabeth Castillo * Swapna Behera
Tezmin Ition Tsai * William S. Peters, Sr.

Now Available

www.innerchildpress.com/the-year-of-the-poet

The Year of the Poet IX
May 2022

Featured Global Poets

Ndaba Sibanda * Smrutiranjan Mohanty
Ajanta Paul * Monalisa Dash Dwibedy

Climate Change and Birds

Poetry . . . Ekphrasticly Speaking

The Poetry Posse 2021

Gail Weston Shazor * Albert Carasco * Hülya N. Yılmaz
Jackie Davis Allen * Caroline Nazareno * Eliza Segiet
Alicja Maria Kuberska * Teresa E. Gallion * Joe Paire
Kimberly Burnham * Shareef Abdur – Rasheed
Ashok K. Bhargava * Elizabeth Castillo * Swapna Behera
Tezmin Ition Tsai * William S. Peters, Sr.

The Year of the Poet IX
June 2022

Featured Global Poets

Yuan Changming * Azeezat Okunlola
Tanja Ajtlé * Philip Chijioke Abonyi

Climate Change and Trees

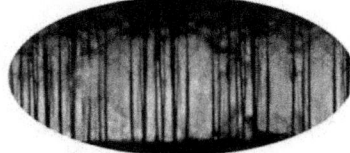

Poetry . . . Ekphrasticly Speaking

The Poetry Posse 2022

Gail Weston Shazor * Albert Carasco * Hülya N. Yılmaz
Jackie Davis Allen * Caroline Nazareno * Eliza Segiet
Alicja Maria Kuberska * Teresa E. Gallion * Joe Paire
Kimberly Burnham * Shareef Abdur – Rasheed
Ashok K. Bhargava * Elizabeth Castillo * Swapna Behera
Tezmin Ition Tsai * William S. Peters, Sr.

The Year of the Poet IX
July 2022

Featured Global Poets

Michelle Joan Barulich * Mili Das
Anna Ferriero * Ujjal Mandal

Climate Change and Animals

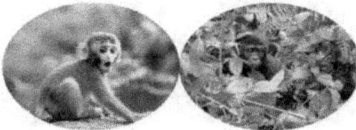

Poetry . . . Ekphrasticly Speaking

The Poetry Posse 2022

Gail Weston Shazor * Albert Carasco * Hülya N. Yılmaz
Jackie Davis Allen * Caroline Nazareno * Eliza Segiet
Alicja Maria Kuberska * Teresa E. Gallion * Joe Paire
Kimberly Burnham * Shareef Abdur – Rasheed
Ashok K. Bhargava * Elizabeth Castillo * Swapna Behera
Tezmin Ition Tsai * William S. Peters, Sr.

The Year of the Poet IX
August 2022

Featured Global Poets

Pankhuri Sinha * Abdulloh Abdumominov
Caroline Turunç * Tali Cohen Shabtai

Climate Change and Agriculture

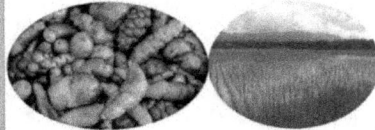

Poetry . . . Ekphrasticly Speaking

The Poetry Posse 2022

Gail Weston Shazor * Albert Carasco * Hülya N. Yılmaz
Jackie Davis Allen * Caroline Nazareno * Eliza Segiet
Alicja Maria Kuberska * Teresa E. Gallion * Joe Paire
Kimberly Burnham * Shareef Abdur – Rasheed
Ashok K. Bhargava * Elizabeth Castillo * Swapna Behera
Tezmin Ition Tsai * William S. Peters, Sr.

Now Available

www.innerchildpress.com/the-year-of-the-poet

The Year of the Poet IX
September 2022

Featured Global Poets

Ngozi Olivia Osuoha * Biswajit Mishra
Sylwia K. Malinowska * Sajid Hussein

Climate Change and Wind and Weather Patterns

Poetry . . . Ekphrasticly Speaking

The Poetry Posse 2022

Gail Weston Shazor * Albert Carasco * Hülya N. Yılmaz
Jackie Davis Allen * Caroline Nazareno * Eliza Segiet
Alicja Maria Kubenska * Teresa E. Gallion * Joe Paire
Kimberly Burnham * Shareef Abdur - Rasheed
Ashok K. Bhargava * Elizabeth Castillo * Swapna Behera
Tezmin Ition Tsai * William S. Peters, Sr.

The Year of the Poet IX
October 2022

Featured Global Poets

Andrew Kouroupos * Brenda Mohammed
Carthornia Kouroupos * Faleeha Hassan

Climate Change and Oil and Power

Poetry . . . Ekphrasticly Speaking

The Poetry Posse 2022

Gail Weston Shazor * Albert Carasco * Hülya N. Yılmaz
Jackie Davis Allen * Caroline Nazareno * Eliza Segiet
Alicja Maria Kubenska * Teresa E. Gallion * Joe Paire
Kimberly Burnham * Shareef Abdur – Rasheed
Ashok K. Bhargava * Elizabeth Castillo * Swapna Behera
Tezmin Ition Tsai * William S. Peters, Sr.

The Year of the Poet IX
November 2022

Featured Global Poets

Hema Ravi * Shafkat Aziz Hajam
Selma Kopic * Ibrahim Honjo

Climate Change : Time to Act

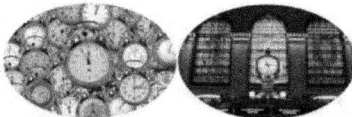

Poetry . . . Ekphrasticly Speaking

The Poetry Posse 2022

Gail Weston Shazor * Albert Carasco * Hülya N. Yılmaz
Jackie Davis Allen * Caroline Nazareno * Eliza Segiet
Alicja Maria Kubenska * Teresa E. Gallion * Joe Paire
Kimberly Burnham * Shareef Abdur – Rasheed
Ashok K. Bhargava * Elizabeth Castillo * Swapna Behera
Tezmin Ition Tsai * William S. Peters, Sr.

The Year of the Poet IX
December 2022

Featured Global Poets

Elarbi Abdelfattah * Lorraine Cragg
Neha Bhandarkar * Robert Gibbons

Climate Change Bees, Butterflies and Insect Life

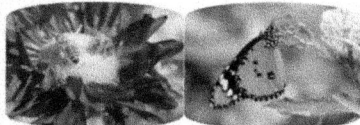

Poetry . . . Ekphrasticly Speaking

The Poetry Posse 2022

Gail Weston Shazor * Albert Carasco * Hülya N. Yılmaz
Jackie Davis Allen * Caroline Nazareno * Eliza Segiet
Alicja Maria Kubenska * Teresa E. Gallion * Joe Paire
Kimberly Burnham * Shareef Abdur – Rasheed
Ashok K. Bhargava * Elizabeth Castillo * Swapna Behera
Tezmin Ition Tsai * William S. Peters, Sr.

Now Available

www.innerchildpress.com/the-year-of-the-poet

The Year of the Poet X
January 2023
Featured Global Poets
JuNe Barefield * Swayam Prashant
Willow Rose * Shabbirhusein K Jamnagerwalla

Children : Difference Makers

Iqbal Masih

The Poetry Posse 2023

Gail Weston Shazor * Albert Carasco * Hülya N. Yılmaz
Jackie Davis Allen * Caroline Nazareno * Kimberly Burnham
Alicja Maria Kuberska * Teresa E. Gallion * Joe Paire
Michelle Joan Barulich * Shareef Abdur – Rasheed
Ashok K. Bhargava * Elizabeth Castillo * Swapna Behera
Tezmin Ition Tsai * Eliza Segiet * William S. Peters, Sr.

The Year of the Poet X
February 2023
Featured Global Poets
Christena Williams * Hilda Graciela Kraft
Francesco Favetta * Dr. H.C. Louise Hudon

Children : Difference Makers

Ruby Bridges

The Poetry Posse 2023

Gail Weston Shazor * Albert Carasco * Hülya N. Yılmaz
Jackie Davis Allen * Caroline Nazareno * Kimberly Burnham
Alicja Maria Kuberska * Teresa E. Gallion * Joe Paire
Michelle Joan Barulich * Shareef Abdur – Rasheed
Ashok K. Bhargava * Elizabeth Castillo * Swapna Behera
Tezmin Ition Tsai * Eliza Segiet * William S. Peters, Sr.

The Year of the Poet X
March 2023
Featured Global Poets
Clarena Martinez Turizo * Binod Dawadi
Til Kumari Sharma * Petrouchka Alexieva

Children : Difference Makers

Yo Yo Ma

The Poetry Posse 2023

Gail Weston Shazor * Albert Carasco * Hülya N. Yılmaz
Jackie Davis Allen * Caroline Nazareno * Kimberly Burnham
Alicja Maria Kuberska * Teresa E. Gallion * Joe Paire
Michelle Joan Barulich * Shareef Abdur – Rasheed
Ashok K. Bhargava * Elizabeth Castillo * Swapna Behera
Tezmin Ition Tsai * Eliza Segiet * William S. Peters, Sr.

The Year of the Poet X
April 2023
Featured Global Poets
Maxwanette A Poetess * Alonzo Gross
Türkan Ergör * Ibrahim Honjo

Children : Difference Makers

Claudette Colvin

The Poetry Posse 2023

Gail Weston Shazor * Albert Carasco * Hülya N. Yılmaz
Jackie Davis Allen * Caroline Nazareno * Kimberly Burnham
Alicja Maria Kuberska * Teresa E. Gallion * Joe Paire
Michelle Joan Barulich * Shareef Abdur – Rasheed
Ashok K. Bhargava * Elizabeth Castillo * Swapna Behera
Tezmin Ition Tsai * Eliza Segiet * William S. Peters, Sr.

Now Available

www.innerchildpress.com/the-year-of-the-poet

Now Available

and there is much, much more !

visit . . .

www.innerchildpress.com/antho
logies-sales-special.php

Also check out our Authors and
all the wonderful Books
Available at :

www.innerchildpress.com/autho
rs-pages

World Healing World Peace
2020

Poets for Humanity

Now Available

www.worldhealingworldpeacepoetry.com

INNER CHILD PRESS

WORLD HEALING WORLD PEACE

2018

A Poetry Anthology for Humanity

Now Available

www.worldhealingworldpeacepoetry.com

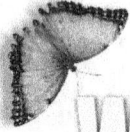

I support

World Healing
World Peace

www.worldhealingworldpeacepoetry.com

230

World Healing World Peace

i am a believer!

World Healing World Peace

2012, 2014, 2016, 2018, 2020

Now Available

www.worldhealingworldpeacepoetry.com

231

Inner Child Press International

'building bridges of cultural understanding'

Meet our Cultural Ambassadors

Fakredin Shehu
Director of Cultural

Faleha Hassan
Iraq - USA

Elizabeth E. Castillo
Philippines

Antoinette Coleman
Chicago
Midwest USA

Ananda Nepali
Nepal - Tibet
Northern India

Kimberly Burnham
Pacific Northwest
USA

Alicja Kuberska
Poland
Eastern Europe

Swapna Behera
India
Southeast Asia

Kolade O. Freedom
Nigeria
West Africa

Mansif Beroual
Morroco
Northern Africa

Ashok K. Bhargava
Canada

Tzemin Ition Tsai
Republic of China
Greater China

Alicia M. Ramírez
Mexico
Central America

Christena AV Williams
Jamaica
Caribbean

Louise Hudon
Eastern Europe

Aziz Mountassir
Morocco
Northern Africa

Shareef Abdur-Rasheed
Southeastern USA

Laure Charazac
France
Western Europe

Mohammad Ikbal Harb
Lebanon
Middle East

Mohamed Abdel
Aziz Shmeis
Egypt
Middle East

Hilary Mainga
Kenya
Eastern Africa

Josephus R. Johnson
Liberia

www.innerchildpress.com

This Anthological Publication
is underwritten solely by

Inner Child Press International

Inner Child Press is a Publishing Company
Founded and Operated by Writers. Our
personal publishing experiences provides
us an intimate understanding of the
sometimes daunting challenges Writers,
New and Seasoned may face in the
Business of Publishing and Marketing
their Creative "Written Work".

For more Information

Inner Child Press International

www.innerchildpress.com

'building bridges of cultural understanding'

202 Wiltree Court, State College, Pennsylvania 16801

www.innerchildpress.com

~ fini ~

www.ingramcontent.com/pod-product-compliance
Lightning Source LLC
LaVergne TN
LVHW022321080426
835508LV00041B/1690